Spiritual Principles in Strategic Alliances

Transform Status Quo Mediocrity into Greatness

Joe Kittel
SPiBR.org LLC

Copyright © 2012 SPiBR.org LLC   All rights reserved

ISBN 978-0-9881858-0-7

Printed and bound in the United States of America. All rights reserved. No part of this book may be reproduced in any form or by any electronic or mechanical means including information storage and retrieval systems without permission in writing from the copyright holder, except by a reviewer who may quote brief passages in review. The scanning, uploading and distribution of this book via the Internet or via any other means without the permission of the publisher is illegal and punishable by law. Please purchase only authorized electronic editions, and do not participate in or encourage electronic piracy of copyrighted materials. Your support of the author's rights is appreciated.

Limits of Liability and Disclaimer of Warranty

The author and publisher shall not be liable for your misuse of this material. This book is strictly for informational and educational purposes.

Warning – Disclaimer

The purpose of this book is to educate and entertain. The author and/or publisher do not guarantee that anyone following these techniques, suggestions, tips, ideas, or strategies will become successful. The author and/or publisher shall have neither liability nor responsibility to anyone with respect to any loss or damage caused, or alleged to be caused, directly or indirectly by the information contained in this book.

Original manuscript edited by Margette Pulis, The Bottomline.
Published book edited by Erin Martineau, Refiners Eye LLC.
Cover design and typesetting by Susan Veach.
Illustrations by Rand Kruback.

*Your daily life is your temple and your religion.
Whenever you enter into it take with you your all.*

— *The Prophet* by Kahlil Gibran

About SPiBR.org LLC

Founded in 2007 in Loveland, Colorado, SPiBR.org LLC is an international consultancy focused on strategic alliance managers. We are about the practical application of spiritual principles in business relationships. We help strategic alliance managers increase personal and organizational effectiveness and create a more value-enabling climate. Professional services include training, consulting and coaching services for alliance managers, alliance management effectiveness, and transformational practices.

www.SPiBR.org

Acknowledgements

As you perceive the holy companions who travel with you, you will realize that there is no journey, but only an awakening.

— A Course in Miracles

I am grateful for the loving support and encouragement I have received from many individuals. Here are some of my holy companions who have been with me on this journey; some for a few years, some for many years, and a few for a lifetime: Anna Bedolla, Paul Beiser, Karl-Peter Bender, Genevieve "Twirly" Bond, Bridget Booth, Scott Brackett, Barbara Campbell, Art Canter, Astrid Claßen, Alan Cooke, Larry Denmark, Ard-Pieter de Man, Geert Duysters, Hanoch Eiron, Gianni Ercolani, Torsten Geers, Jörg Gerlach, Pam Goodell, Kevin Henshaw, Sharon Hronek, Brian Hyodo, Mike Hudson, Jonathan Hughes, Andrea Isaacs, Cindy Jackson, David Karchere, Sara Keen, Aaron Kittel, Allie Kittel (especially her harp music – helpful as I wrote), Jen Kittel, Mike Kittel, Richard Kittel, Robert Kittel, Sue Kittel, Jonny Klasson, Gwen Knight, Ned Koss, Akila Kumar, Volker Kyra, David Lesser, Art Lewandowski, Gordo Long, Ralph Lucero, Erin Martineau, Jean McWeeney, Tim Mikkelsen, Kathe Molly, Mike Nevin, Rand Newman, Beverly Olson-Dopffel, Wolfgang Oskierski, Nick Palmer, Tom Pitner, Ulrich Porst, Quentin Price, Cliff Pulis, Margette Pulis, Carol Rehme, Robby Robbins, Hans-Ulrich Schaller, Alexandra Schweitzer, Robyn Shean, Brad Slaten, Klaus Steiner, Nadine St Gemme, Tim Tillson, Laura Visioni, John Voelker, Norma Watenpaugh, Jeff Weiss and Kirk Wilkinson.

A few individuals deserve special acknowledgement. Scott Brakkett is a brother in spirit and fellow experienced alliance manager, who has encouraged me along this path for many, many years. Larry Denmark remains a spiritual father to me, helping me awaken and find a new way to live. Kirk Wilkinson, my last manager at Hewlett-Packard (HP), taught me gratitude and provided unconditional enthusiasm for these bold ideas in alliancing. Hanoch

Eiron, a dear friend and experienced alliance manager, gave of his time and energy critiquing nearly all of this material and providing numerous insightful suggestions. Art Lewandowski came into my life at just the right time, carried just the right message and helped rescue our van in Philly. My first editor, Margette Pulis, painstakingly helped me verbalize these ideas. Erin Martineau provided her editing expertise that helped me further refine the book for publication. Vantage Partners' partners and consultants provided clear value to my alliance work at HP and have encouraged me the past many years, especially Jeff, Jon, Sara and Laura. The Narcotics Anonymous (NA) fellowship has been a practical spiritual university for a few decades; obviously, those individuals go unnamed, but they know who they are. My other spiritual university, Friedreich's Ataxia, (FA) is embodied in two of my four children, Aaron and Allie. My wife of over a third of a century and the loving mother of our four children, Sue, gave me the original encouragement in July 2005 to leave HP, to write this book and to start living my dream. And Andrea Isaacs is currently helping me in so many ways to live my dream, to live a life beyond my wildest dreams.

> *When the student is ready the teacher will appear.*
> *When the teacher is ready the student will appear.*
> *And when the student is really ready he will realize*
> *The Teacher is with him always and everywhere.*
>
> — The Teacher

Excerpts from this book have been selected and published as an *ASAP Best Practice Bulletin*, a monthly membership bulletin for the *Association of Strategic Alliance Professionals* (**www.strategic-alliances.org**).

*This book is dedicated to those who regularly
do the impossible with nothing in the eye of a hurricane.
You know who you are.*

Note: If you would like to see the book's Figures (illustrations) in color, or if some of the illustrations are hard to read, you can download them all at:

www.spibr.org/bookillustrations.pdf.

CONTENTS	PAGE

1. **INTRODUCTION** 1
    Spiritual Disclaimer 1
    Target Audience: experienced strategic alliance managers 2
    The Purpose of This Book 3
    The Audience's Points-of-View 3
    Experiencing Transformation 5
    Focus on Our Most Important *and* Our Most Difficult Challenges 8

2. **STRATEGIC ALLIANCES (PROBLEM I)** 11
    Definition 11
    The Best Proving Ground for Business Relationship Effectiveness 11
    Complexities 13
    Other Difficulties 14
    Strategic Alliancing Trends 18
    Summary 18

3. **MOST STRATEGIC ALLIANCES FAIL. WHY? (PROBLEM II)** 19
    Failure in Relationship 19
    Zero-Sum Scarcity Mindsets – a poor environment 20
    Lack of Trust – no foundation 23
    Relationship Naïveté – traditional business does not know any better .. 24
    Could It Be The People? – if so, just tell them, "relate better" 27
    Unconscious-Incompetence –
    lack of real awareness can lead to harmful results 28
    Poor Communication –
    over-communication is poor communication 29
    Organization Addictions to Complexity and Drama –
    the "yeah, buts …" 30
    High-Technology, Industry-Specific Challenges –
    ADHD and proud of it 32
    Summary 33

4. **FOCUS ON PERSONAL *AND* ALLIANCE SUCCESS (SOLUTION I – INSIGHTS)** 35
    Personal Success Factors – the framework 36

Alliance Success Factors – bring our substance to bear 38
Knowledge – affects <15% of personal success............................ 44
Skills – affects <30% of personal success 47
Attitude & Mindset – affects 55-85% of personal success 52
The Insightful Intersect –
Relationship & People | Attitude & Mindset................................ 58
Summary.. 61

5. ROLE CLARITY – WHO AM I? (PROBLEM OR SOLUTION) 63

Lack of Role Clarity Adversely Affects Success Rate................................. 64
A Singularly Unique Job 65
Traditional Default Assumptions – problematic role comparisons 67
Unhealthy Value-Stifling Behaviors – problem 70
Value-Limiting Traps – problem 74
The Negotiator Role – a pervasive solution.. 78
A "Mini-CEO" – a concretely limiting solution 79
Agents of Change – adaptive solution.. 82
Our Relationship with (the Attributes of) Deity –
a thoughtful solution, leading to grandeur... 88
Negotiating with Your Greatest Spiritual Teacher –
Negotiating with the Infinite 91
Suggested Job Description – be a focused solution................................... 93

6. THE POWER IN SIMPLE TRUTHS (SOLUTION II – AUTHENTIC EFFECTIVENESS) 99

Simplicity 99
The Truth 100
Fundamental Principles 101
Spirituality – improving attitude & mindset, deepening relationship .. 102
Question: Are We Talking About Religion? Answer: Yes *and* No 106
Two Thought Systems –
ego-based or spirit-based, in fear or in love 108
Oneness – no separation between people,
no duality of thought, integrity... 109
Now – to be fully present in each instant of time,
one eternal now, eternity.. 111

We Are Divine – see the greatness at our core,
in everyone, in everything 113

We Create – based on our divine nature, thought is cause 114

Love – the universal force which compels growth; enthusiasm,
inspiration, joy 116

Assessing and Changing Attitude & Mindset 117

7. **THE VALUE OF SPIRITUALITY IN BUSINESS RELATIONSHIPS (IMPACT) 123**

Personal Value 123

The ROI of Spirituality in Strategic Alliances 130

Alliance Climate Change 132

Business Transformation 132

Alliance Managers –
spearheads of collaborative growth 133

8. **SOME SPIRITUAL PRACTICES IN STRATEGIC ALLIANCING (SOLUTION III) 135**

Presence – mindfulness, the lie of
multi-tasking, be present or be gone 135

Awareness – listen holistically, listen to the collective, see the flow 138

Be Lovingly Confrontational –
shine your light with love and precision 143

Be an Illuminating Mirror – see the good and reflect it back 151

Focus Collective Attention on Value –
opportunities, problems, answers, ecosystem 154

Negotiate – open, trust-filled and focused;
just-enough, just-in-time preparation 167

Self-Obsolescence – giving and receiving are one; always *be* value 173

Transforming an Alliance into a Productive Community –
an attractive home 179

Be the Metaphor for Metamorphosis – *be* the change 184

It Is All About Relationship – the spirit's home 186

9. **CONCLUSION – A CALL TO ACTION – BE FOCUSED, BE BOLD, BE … 187**

Spirituality Addresses Root Cause of Alliance Failure 187

Summary: simplicity, relationship, presence & awareness, attitude & mindset, love 188
Be the Metaphor for Metamorphosis 189
If Not Us, Who? If Not Now, When? 189
Suggested Daily Top Fives 192

10. **APPENDIX** **193**
    Key Terms 193
    Books Along My Path 196
    Thoughts on Metrics 198
    Thoughts on Meditation 202
    Thoughts on Two Thought Systems 206
    Thoughts on Time 213
    Biography 216

REFERENCES (Endnotes) **219**

1. Introduction

The overlap of *spirituality* with *strategic alliance work* becomes clear and obvious when we look past the drama and complexity of both to the simple essence in each.[1] At their core both spirituality and alliancing are about *relationship* – the deepening of relationship.

Most alliances fail. They fail because businesses fail at *relationship*. The need to use spiritual principles in alliance management is clearly a strategic imperative. Our challenge is *how* to bring these principles into business in a practical and non-divisive manner. This book is about the practical application of spiritual principles to help make alliance managers more effective and their alliances more successful in value-creation.[2] In short, this book is about increasing the effectiveness of an alliance, based on a fundamental change in perspective – a change in how we choose to see ourselves, others and situations.

This book describes spiritual principles in a manner palatable to business and practical in alliancing work.[3] We suggest helpful practices that will transform us as alliance managers and transform our alliances. This work calls for boldness and courage; but we already embody such attributes if we are experienced alliance managers. Now we take our bold courageousness to a deeper level for value-enabling benefit. Now we look deeply within ourselves.

Some have described this book as an internal technical manual for strategic alliance managers.

Spiritual Disclaimer

I describe my spirituality as being open and growing; and yet, I acknowledge that I have unseen biases or blind spots that can cause me to be closed-minded. I describe the two "spiritual universities" in my life as my recovery from drug addiction and dealing with my children's progressive disability.[4] I am also a longstanding student of *A Course in Miracles* and an active participant in 12-step recovery (Alcoholics Anonymous and Narcotics

Anonymous).[5] In my writings and in my life, I am very clear about the spiritual principles, or "simple truths," which are important to me.[6] Sometimes my bold clarity coupled with a passion for life can be perceived as zealotry or dogmatism, which I am strongly opposed to. Do *not* blindly accept my simple truths as yours. You have the truth within you; so, *be true to yourself.*

Don't be trapped by dogma —
which is living with the results of other people's thinking.

— Steve Jobs

Please do not blindly accept what I say to be true. Try it out and validate it with your own life experience. Most of the ideas in this book can stand on their own without the need to understand or embrace spiritual principles. As I see it, spirituality sheds light on *why* or *how* this stuff works, and it helps us understand the *fundamental principles* in strategic alliances.

Target Audience:
experienced strategic alliance managers

This book is written *by* and *for* experienced strategic alliance managers, as well as for others involved in the day-to-day operation of an alliance. The reader of this book should have substantial experience in strategic alliances and is looking to make fundamental breakthroughs.[7] They are seeking to understand the fundamentals in alliancing by asking, "How do alliances really work? What can I do to help make my alliance better, to help make it great? How can I be of greater service?"

There is so much at stake in any alliance. Yet, there is often so much chaos, drama, complexity and confusion. Simple clarity and boldness are needed to cut through this obscuring haze. We don't have the time to "mince words." So this book is as bold, clear and direct as possible.

My hope is that this book will be for you a spirituality-in-alliancing primer, something I wish I had 20 years ago.

The Purpose of This Book

This book encourages and emboldens alliance managers to confront our most vexing, strategically important and rewarding issues.[8] It motivates us to *go within* and work on our *most* important strategic alliance of all – our *relationship with our Self*.[9]

This book paints a clear, rational and compelling picture for the *practical* application of spiritual principles, which *do* improve strategic alliances. This book deals directly with changes in attitude & mindset in order to deepen and improve relationship. Relationship work is sorely needed in strategic alliances. And deepening relationship is what spirituality is all about.

What the world of business needs is a fundamental transformation, first by transforming self, then our alliance, then other business relationships, and, in time, the world of business.[10] All transformation starts *within* and then moves *without*. The value-enabling results are greater trust, more open communication, a healthier atmosphere, more creative brainstorming of ideas, and greater collaboration, leading to increased value-creation. We see these results first around ourselves, then in our alliance and, in time, throughout business and the world. We are about changing the world by *being* that change. We are about being the metaphor for metamorphosis.

This difficult and important work is done *in the midst* – in the between. This is work done *between* companies, *between* individuals, *between* mind and heart, and even *between* ideas. Opportunities live *in the midst*. Opportunities are hidden behind the obstacles that are also *in the midst*. The answers to the obstacles which are hiding valuable opportunities are found *in the midst*. And, it's no wonder that all of this is true because spirit lives in the between, *in the midst*, arguably spirit *is* the midst.

The Audience's Points-of-View

Here may be your points-of-view:
- Strategic alliances are *increasingly important* to businesses;

yet, they *continue failing* at an unacceptably high rate (over half fail to achieve their expected value).

- Strategic alliances are difficult and complex. Businesses often do not understand the unique *type* of work nor the *amount* of work required for success.
- Implementing alliancing-related processes, tools and systems in the organization is helpful but insufficient to significantly improve today's abysmal success rates.
- Knowledge acquisition and skills development is also helpful but insufficient; something else is needed. Skills and knowledge alone do not seem to address the fundamental issues.
- Perhaps what's needed is a change in attitude & mindset. But how is this change achieved? And is this type of change even possible?
- Spirituality is too abstract, too religious and too mystical. It has no practical value in the real world of business.
- Bringing up the topic of spirituality in our meetings will bring with it pro- or anti-religious zealotry, and this will be more divisive than helpful.
- Business is no place for spiritual stuff. I am skeptical that spirituality will help. I think it will hurt more than it will help and I already have enough problems.
- I would love to bring spirituality into my work; the connection seems obvious. But *how* can I do that?

Have the above points captured your thoughts around the possible application of spirituality principles in strategic alliances? This emotionally charged objective needs to be dealt with in a rational and objective manner. Such is one of the main purposes of this book.

Introduction

Experiencing Transformation

This book focuses on transformation – yours and your alliance's. What has been my transformation? Below is an overview of alliance-related growth I have experienced over the past 25-30 years. My hope is that my *transformational* experiences might help illustrate *our* potential for grandeur; this phrase may sound grandiose.[11] Transformation is "*both* all about me *and* nothing about me" – it is all about "*we.*" It is about transforming status quo mediocrity into greatness.

It is my hope that through my experiences you might more clearly see your transformational potential. For 16 years I established, developed and managed strategic alliances for Hewlett-Packard (HP) with nearly every high-technology company and in nearly every form of intercompany business relationship.[12] Here are some highlights:

- From 1989 to 1991, I helped establish and lead a three-year, multi-million dollar strategic alliance with US West Advanced Technology (now Qwest Communications, a 14 billion dollar telecommunications company covering most of the western U.S.). This alliance focused on collaboratively developing advanced object-oriented software development technology. Each year engineers from one company relocated and worked in the lab of the other company. This was my first strategic alliance.

- In March 1997, I was part of the core team that established HP's corporate-level strategic alliance with Microsoft. Our directive was to simplify computing for enterprise customers (large corporations). I helped prepare HP's senior executives with briefings on intercompany issues: organizational, strategic and cultural differences.[13] I led the intercompany negotiations on UNIX/NT-interoperability – the most strategically contentious area of that corporate-level alliance. Then for three years, I coordinated over 125 technology initiatives between the two companies, often directly leading negotiations on behalf of HP's business units, such as internet

Spiritual Principles in Strategic Alliances

security and cryptography, objective-oriented software and UNIX/NT interoperability. Today this alliance impacts nearly every part of HP's business and is measured in many billions of dollars per year.

- From 2002 to 2005, I established the first strategic alliance between HP's printing business (IPG) and SAP.[14] The catalyst deal for this alliance was valued at over 300 million dollars during HP's business planning horizon. This relationship was focused on co-developing enterprise document workflow technology for integration into SAP's application integration middleware, SAP NetWeaver. Many had considered this deal to be impossible. It was during this time when I was explicitly searching for spiritual principles in alliances. It took 18 months of intense discussion and nine months of formal contract negotiation to close the deal. Today SAP leverages in excess of one billion dollars in HP/IPG product and services each year.

Over this 16-year period I experienced, personified and observed the complexities, challenges and failures discussed throughout this book. I also achieved significant success and growth. Success outweighed failure, and so HP allowed me to continue working as a strategic alliance manager.[15] I can look back now and see how my alliancing career evolved through four types of change agents: fact-based, authority-based, relationship-based and transformational.[16]

In my earliest alliancing work I over-analyzed and over-drove. I prepared for negotiations with excruciating detail. We often lost sight of the big picture as we examined various terms into the minutia. Being a driver-driver personality type, "*my*" alliance was not a fun place to work – for me or anyone else. "No deal" was not an option. I heard second-hand that others in the organization feared that I might die from a heart attack, based on my obsessive intensity. At the conclusion of some especially intense negotiations with IBM, an HP coworker suggested that my business card should have the title "Asshole Negotiator."[17] At the time I interpreted his comment as a compliment; an admission that I was more competitively successful than he. Now I see this period of my life as dominated by a "*me* vs. you," fear-based world view. I was an excessively-competitive, overly-analytical egomaniac.[18]

Sixteen years later, after *we* had established HP/IPG's first strategic alliance with SAP, others in the alliance (in both companies) had a much different experience working in *our* alliance. I again heard second-hand comments. This time I was described as a "peacemaker" and the "savior of the business." Our negotiations were based on two *simple* slides which captured the essence in the alliance – incremental value and value-impediments.[19] Rather than *making* this alliance happen, we *let* it happen. There were times when it appeared the deal might not happen, and I was willing to accept that outcome. "No deal" was okay.

My 16-year personal transformation was driven by work experiences, but most poignantly by life experiences. Over this same period of time, roughly 1989 through 2005, I *had* to grow. Life seemed to say "grow or die." Two diseases propelled me, often kicking and screaming, through the *acceptance* and then the *embracement* phases of spiritual growth. Sometimes life drags me kicking and screaming to precisely where I truly want to be.

My disease was the disease of drug addiction. Until I could learn to completely accept my addiction, I was stuck in the disease. With *acceptance* came *transcendence*, "freedom from active addiction." Over considerable time I continued growing, next through embracement. With loving *embracement* (acceptance combined with love) comes *transformation*. I now gratefully realize that my disease of addiction is *the greatest spiritual blessing in my life*. It has forced me to wake up and stay awake. I had to "figure out this stuff or die" – in a literal, spiritual and practical sense. For me, spirituality is not a theoretical academic debate. It is a life and death matter, here and now. I learned in Narcotics Anonymous that if something is not practical it is not spiritual.

During this same period of time, our family had to learn to *accept* and then *embrace* a physical disease that afflicts two of our four children, Friedreich's Ataxia (FA). FA slowly destroys bodies and shortens their lives.[20] This disease affects my oldest son and my youngest daughter. Like addiction, FA also affects our entire family and the community of friends and family around us. This disease has forced me to stay in the moment, see the oneness of us all, and it has taught me that we are not our bodies. With acceptance and embracement I am continually taught amazing lessons from both diseases.

Some might say that having these two diseases in one life is "just not fair." But life is not fair. I actually have two spiritual "universities" which, if I remain open, continually teach me valuable lessons. I have learned from my disease and my children's disease simple and practical spiritual truths. These simple truths come into my work life and provide me with an unfair *competitive* advantage. But does competition really have any place in a spiritual practice? Is there such a thing as "competitive spirituality"? Well, I believe the competitive aspect of spirituality is experienced as *inspiration*.[21]

Inspiration provides a transformational competitive advantage. It is my hope that this book will inspire you to be grand and transform you and your world.

Focus on Our Most Important *and* Our Most Difficult Challenges

There is something exciting and inspiring when we focus on achieving important and challenging accomplishments. Let's explore the intersection of our most important and challenging aspects of our work as strategic alliance managers.

Strategic alliances are *critically important* in business and they are *extraordinarily difficult*. We are trying to get *competitive* companies to *collaborate*. The very nature of our work requires us to face important and challenging issues. Our companies and our success depend upon us proactively facing and dealing with difficult issues, head on. Maybe it is *challenge* itself that attracts us to this type of work.

Focus on fundamentals – trying to understand root-cause or fundamental issues is of paramount importance in solving difficult problems. My schooling in electrical engineering actually made me enthusiastic for fundamental principles. I actually loved calculus and physics; their fundamental principles amazed me. Decades passed before I could clearly appreciate the attractive nature of fundamental principles:

- They **coalesce** and **clarify** prior experiences, providing insight and **inspiration**.
- They **expand** our problem-solving and **creative abilities**. They **enthuse** us.
- They bring a **predictive** ability. With a sense of **timelessness** they allow us to see the **interconnectedness** of events and to see how the future might unfold.

Focus on relationships – relationship is *the* fundamental issue in alliancing. Relationships are a root-cause source of alliance success or failures. Deepening relationship *is* the answer. Central in relationships is spirituality – the deepening of our relationship with others, the Infinite and Self.[22]

Talking about spirituality in business is difficult. But remember, as alliance managers we do not shirk from difficult issues; so, we should not avoid spirituality, *if* it will be *helpful*. This book will show that spirituality *does* help:

- **Transform** ourselves and our alliance.
- Allow for more **open** and **trust-filled communications**.
- **Deepen** and, therefore, **improve relationships** – interpersonal and intercompany.
- **Change the overall climate** in our alliance.[23]

Focus on attitude & mindset – in order to use spirituality to deepen relationships, we need to deal with our own and others' attitudes & mindsets. This is our most difficult and most valuable work.

Focus on the dauntingly impossible – each one of these topics – alliancing, relationships, spirituality, attitude & mindset – are individually very difficult. In combination, they are daunting, arguably impossible. Alliancing is about "doing the impossible with nothing." Improving relationships is really hard work. Talking about spirituality in business is nearly taboo. Going within self to do spiritual work brings up deep-seated and life-long fears. And many people believe that changing attitude & mindset is impossible.

Alone we face impossible odds. Together we *do* the impossible, as a *"we* thing." *That is* an alliance.

> *The impossible often has a kind of integrity which the merely improbable lacks.*
> — Douglas Adams

2. Strategic Alliances (Problem I)

This chapter defines strategic alliance and indicates the extraordinary challenges we face as alliance managers, as we lead the establishment, development and management of relationships within the alliance.

Definition

A strategic alliance is a **long-term value-creating** business relationship. These relationships last beyond the typical 3-5 year planning horizon of most companies. Their *primary* purpose is to *create* value. This value is created in *tangible* forms like incremental revenue,[24] a new product or technology, better solutions, or the development of a new market. However, future value is conceived in the *intangible* forms of value like knowledge transfer, organizational learning, increased brand value, improved customer and partner loyalty, risk mitigation or sharing, and new strategic options. Strategic alliances differ from other forms of business relationship, in that they are:

- long-term.
- value-creating.

The Best Proving Ground for Business Relationship Effectiveness

There are other business relationships that may be strategically important, but they are not alliances. Supplier relationships may be critically important, but they are primarily about value-*exchange* and so they are not alliances. If a co-marketing or co-selling relationship is not primarily about *increasing* the value in a solution or creating a new market, it is not a strategic alliance. The point of this simple definition, focused on *time* and *value*, is not to ignore nor trivialize other business relationships. The point is to recognize that strategic alliances are *the most challenging* type of relationship in business. Strategic alliances are about long-term value-creation.

Why are strategic alliances the most challenging type of business relationship and, therefore, our *best proving ground* for understanding and improving value-creating effectiveness? It is because these relationships must grow and evolve through a process that involves a series of unnatural and nearly-impossible phases. These phases are described as follows:

1. **Create value** – first, get two highly-*competitive* companies to *collaborate* and *create* incremental value together. For traditional business this is a challenging and unnatural act, especially considering the predominantly fear-based climate present in most businesses. Creation requires a sense of abundance or love; creation requires a *lack of fear*.

2. **Divide the created value** – dividing up value between companies is a relatively natural act for most businesses. The companies figure out how to parse revenue, technology, intellectual property, or ecosystem layers. However, this act of value division is actually an exercise in scarcity – it is about dividing up a fixed resource; by definition, your win is my loss. This is a fear-based (divisive or scarcity-based) act. It takes us out of the critically important collaborative (or love-based) climate required for value-creation.

3. **Create again** – from value-division the relationship then has to morph back into the unnatural state of value-creation. This traversal from *dividing* value (fear) back to *creating* value (love) is a nearly impossible transformation for any relationship to navigate through. The difficulty of this traversal is attested to in *The Program on Negotiation*. This relationship change is extraordinarily challenging and nearly impossible. This is one of the main reasons why most alliances fail to create value to their fullest potential.

4. **Repeat, long-term** – then, continually go from the unnatural (create) through the nearly-impossible (transition from divide back to create). Create, divide, create, divide

... transformational re-creation. This is *extraordinarily* challenging.

The purpose of business is to *create value*. Businesses today are increasingly turning to business relationships, of all forms, to create this value. As we learn how to fundamentally improve the value-creating effectiveness in strategic alliances, businesses can then use these insights to help improve other business relationships.

Strategic alliances are our best proving grounds for learning how to make relationships more effective.
Lessons learned here can be applied anywhere.

Complexities

Alliances often span the entire lifecycle of product and service development, and delivery. They often impact every area of an organization: Research & Development, Marketing, Sales and Customer Service. Alliances involve resource investments and the management of intellectual property, affecting Finance and Legal departments. Human Resources departments help us deal with unique staffing, personnel development and intercompany recruitment challenges. These stakeholders rightly expect updates on the status of an alliance. Providing useful and often spontaneous updates, to a broad range of constituents is complex and challenging.

As alliance managers, we help companies collaborate. We need to help the people working in the alliance deal with significant cultural and strategic differences that exist between the companies. Such intercompany "chasms" are complex and often present the greatest challenges to effective collaboration. Providing others with practical, easy-to-understand recommendations for dealing with such differences is critically important, and it is hard work.

Adding to organizational, cultural and strategic complexities, we must deal with intricacies in technologies, legal and regulatory issues and complex global value-delivery mechanisms.

Capping this all off are people. Business relationships involve people, and people are complex. The antidote for complexity is simplicity. This point can easily get lost in the midst of the day-to-day complexity, drama and chaos in an alliance.

Other Difficulties

We face difficulties that would be unacceptable in any other area of business. Our *role* as strategic alliance manager is often ill-defined. It rarely reflects the true strategic nature of the opportunities and challenges we face. Often our role is simplistically equated to value-*exchange* roles in business, such as a sales representative or people working in procurement. Those jobs do involve external business relationships. But people in sales and procurement can all too easily overlook both the long-term and value-*creating* aspect of the work, both of which are critical in a strategic alliance. The role of program manager can align with the broad nature of alliance manager and can be value-creative, but program managers often work on *short*-term activities. Such an orientation can end up limiting their ability to fulfill a strategic alliance's fullest value-creative potential.

Role ambiguity places us at odds with the rest of our organization. Others expect us to prioritize on near-term, tangible value at the expense of longer-term returns. Our personal performance measures are nebulous and open to debate. Our objectives vary based on where we reside in an organization and which internal stakeholders most influence our direct line manager. Confusion around our role makes time management nearly impossible – it can be unclear what we *should* do, and what we should *not* do.

We often recognize needs others cannot see. We often have to make unpopular recommendations, based on our unique holistic, long-term perspective. Role ambiguity creates stress as our expectations diverge from that of others.

Our job can be lonely; it is like no other job. A CEO's job is similar in that they span the entire business. But the Board and investors force the CEO to focus primarily on near-term tangible forms of value. The nature of intercompany collaboration requires us to be more patient than a CEO can afford to be. It often takes considerable time before our alliance starts bearing tangible fruit. The greatest difference is that CEO's have direct control over significant resources. We typically have little, if any, resource under our direct control. Most of our work has to be accomplished via the subtle art of influence and persuasion.

Our job as alliance manager is about "doing the impossible with nothing." With insufficient resource and limited organizational power, we get highly-*competitive* companies to *collaborate* in a predominately fear-based climate.

Where can we turn to for help in our unique and lonely job? If we are in a traditional business team, others in that team will find it hard to relate to the uniqueness of our work. Alternatively, we may be part of a centralized team of alliance managers, who are then embedded into traditional business teams. Here, our challenges are different. In this team we are limited as to what information we can share with our peers. Information-sharing is limited by confidentiality restrictions, anti-trust and regulatory constraints. Such legal restrictions define what information we can and cannot share. And, given the other alliance managers are in many ways our personal competitors, how openly will we want to share our most helpful and insightful ideas? What a paradox!

At times our greatest difficulty is actually within *ourselves*. As we grow in experience as an alliance manager we may, at times, find ourselves wrestling with some unhealthy behaviors:

- We are motivated to "drive" the alliance and "make" things happen. However, if we are not careful we can "**over-drive**" the alliance, alienating others and stifling creativity.

- Early on, in an attempt to "control" our alliance, we may become an **information gatekeeper**. The more information flows, the more value can be created; if we try to control the flow of information, making it all pass "through" us, information flow is restricted, which does a disservice to the alliance.

- To help mitigate risk-exposure to our own company we may **overanalyze** situations and over-prepare for negotiations. This adds unnecessary complexity to an already complex job.

Sometimes in the midst of excess complexity, important issues get lost, which increases, rather than decreases, risk-exposure.

- During periods of escalation we may have to dictate. Based on apparent effectiveness we may be tempted to continue being **dictatorial**, long after the escalation is over. But dictators get near-term results at the expense of long-term relations.
- We may think our job is primarily about arranging executive meetings, believing everything happens from the top-down in business. We then **ignore bottom-up** organizational buy-in.
- At times we may exhibit **self-promoting** behaviors, highlighting all of the challenges we have to deal with in order to make our already-tough job seem even tougher. This may help us personally, but at the cost of casting a negative atmosphere over the alliance. This isn't helpful.
- We may emphasize distrustful behavior of the partner, stirring up **excessive drama and fear**. There are companies we "love to fear" (e.g., Microsoft or Wal-Mart); but emphasizing this negative aspect of the partner does a disservice to the effectiveness of the alliance. This drama is a distraction.
- We may continually highlight the **complexity** of our job in order to make ourselves appear more important to others. Complexity for complexity's sake is not useful. It is detrimental. It obscures from sight the simple essence in an alliance – which is all about value. Spotlighting complexity makes it harder for us to see the incremental value in an alliance.

At times our job seems overwhelming. We may feel quite desperate for help.

Strategic Alliances

Figure 2.4 – Are we begging for help? If not, why not?!

*A beggar had been sitting by the side of a road for over thirty years. One day a stranger walked by. "Spare some change?" mumbled the beggar. "I, by myself, have nothing to give you," said the stranger. Then he asked: "What's that you are sitting on?" "Nothing," replied the beggar. "Just an old box. I have been sitting on it for as long as I can remember." "Ever **look inside?**" asked the stranger. "No." said the beggar. "What's the point? There's nothing in there."*
(Note: this story concludes in Chapter 9; don't look ahead!)

- *The Power of Now* by Eckhart Tolle

It seems many of our greatest difficulties start and end with*in* ourselves. Paradoxically such problems are not solved all *by* ourselves. This concept may be difficult to grasp, but it is the basis of our greatest power and effectiveness.

As we wrestle with our internal difficulties, we struggle to find meaningful help. We all need someone to talk with about our work. We need honest feedback when we exhibit unhealthy behavior. We need others who will be a sounding board, provide a sanity check and give us a different perspective when we are in challenging situations. We need someone with whom we can empathetically connect, and who can provide us meaningful encouragement. We need someone to help us be more creative. We need each other. We need trusted others. Life is a "we thing."

Strategic Alliancing Trends

Strategic alliances are growing increasingly important. Since the mid-1980s, the number of corporate alliances has increased 25% per year, accounting now for at least one-third of all corporate revenue. At the same time roughly two-thirds of all alliances fail to achieve their expected incremental value. This "success" rate has not significantly improved over the past decade.[25] It is astounding that businesses tolerate such a situation – an extraordinarily high rate-of-failure in an increasingly important area of business.

Fundamental change is needed.
Business as usual is no longer acceptable.

Summary

The prior discussion on the formidable nature of alliancing may sound disheartening. But experienced alliance managers often *love* their work *because* of these challenges.[26] The unrelenting challenge of this work stretches our creative abilities, compelling us to grow. There is no other job like alliance manager. It is one of the most strategically important and personally rewarding jobs in all of business.

Businesses today stagnate. They struggle to find new ways to create incremental value. The untapped value potential in alliances is staggering. If businesses could reverse the current success/failure rates so that two-thirds of their alliances succeeded, rather than failed, the impact on revenue growth would be huge.

Business today needs to grow beyond the limitations imposed from their past. They need to grow beyond the negative effect that excessive competitiveness has had on business climate. The best place to make these positive changes is in strategic alliances and, ultimately, within alliance managers. Here, the use of value-creating practices is most urgently needed and, here, such practices are, out of necessity, being developed.

3. Most Strategic Alliances Fail. Why? (Problem II)

Reminder: this book is written from the point-of-view of alliance managers – *by* and *for* strategic alliance managers. Others may have differing perspectives on why alliances fail, most notably senior management and business consultants. We hope all will benefit from the bold and clear points-of-view shared in this book.

For the past decade over half of all strategic alliances have failed to achieve their expected value.[27] In 2001, roughly 70% failed; in 2006, this "improved" to a 57% failure rate. In our chosen field of work, we fail more often than we succeed. In high-technology (chips, computers, software, etc.) our failure rate is currently 68%. There seems to be a deep reluctance to directly confront the root causes for these failures.

As experienced alliance managers, we realize the strategic importance of boldly and clearly confronting our most difficult issues; again, this is the approach taken in writing this book. Fundamental change is sorely needed in alliancing. But first we must see the problem clearly.

Why are alliances failing?

Failure in Relationship

In a 2001 survey of 130 companies in various industries, 52% of the participants cited *poor relationship* as the *foremost contributor* to alliance failure.[28] Relationship problems were evidenced in the form of low or no trust and poor communication. In 2006, research pointed to poor relationship as the cause for 40% of the failures. A lack in *traditional* business competencies was responsible for the remaining failures: poor strategy and business planning (37-46%), and bad legal and financial terms and conditions (11-14%).

Increased attention is needed on the topic of *relationship*. In 2001, 54% of the alliance managers surveyed said more should be invested in relationship; in 2006, that percentage *increased* to 62%.

The type of real *relationship* work we are talking about is counterintuitive for most people in business. Relationship is actually a *nontraditional* business competency. But relationship is strategically important in alliances.

What are the root causes for failure in relationship? What can businesses do?

As we answer these questions, it is worth emphasizing two key points: (a) simplicity tends to take us toward the truth[29], and (b) there are countless ways to dissect truth. There are other ways to discuss and understand the causes for relationship failure in strategic alliances. The objective here is to simply raise these critical issues for open and focused discussion.

This chapter is simple, clear, bold and thought-provoking. Admittedly, it is mostly about describing the problem, with some mention of solution.

Zero-Sum Scarcity Mindsets – a poor environment

Winning competitive battles is richly rewarded in business. It forces companies to continue providing better solutions at lower costs. Marketplace winners gain share at the expense of weak competitors. In monopolistic, non-competitive situations, innovation stagnates and the entire ecosystem suffers. So, competition is good, right? Well, not necessarily. There are situations where competition can be quite harmful.

In competition there are winners and losers; your win is my loss. This fosters a scarcity-mentality or zero-sum mindset. Collective attention is focused on dividing up fixed resources. In *The Program on Negotiation,* this is described as a "dividing the pie" mindset.[30] The "pie" label may mislead us into thinking that this is an unimportant matter. However, recognizing the all-too-subtle signs of a "divide the pie" versus "expand the pie" mindset is crucial in assessing the atmosphere in our alliance. When this atmosphere slips into a "divide the pie" state, it is *nearly impossible* to switch back to a "pie-expanding" or value-creating mode. Once we start competing, it is *very difficult* to switch back into a climate where collaboration is even possible.

In Jim Collins' book *Good to Great*, the title of the first chapter and the first line of text read:

Good is the enemy of great.

Competition's impact *in* an alliance epitomizes Collins' idea. Competition as perceived in the traditional world of business is good. However, *in* an alliance this good thing becomes the enemy of its greatness. The goodness of competition is the enemy of value-creating collaboration and inspiration. This is not to devalue the importance of competition at all. It is, however, a clear statement that a competitive climate between companies in the nontraditional context of a value-creating strategic alliance is incredibly toxic; competition kills collaboration. A competitive climate will ultimately kill an alliance.

Experienced alliance managers often see subtle but distressing signs of a scarcity mindset exhibited by individuals throughout their organization. We often see deeply held tendencies surface while we are trying to develop an alliance.

As alliance managers we see the potent value-creating vision for our alliance. We work hard to help others see that long-term potential. As we continue working to bring this vision to fruition, we sometimes hear subtly disconcerting questions from our own management team:

- What are the *gives* and *gets* in this alliance? What are we *giving* and *getting* back in return?
- What is the *balance of trade*? This alliance had better be balanced.
- Are our *needs* being taken care of?

To most people in business these questions are not only rational, they are necessary. They would argue that these questions *need* to be answered. These questions make absolute sense from a competitively-oriented perspective. However, the mere *asking* of these questions is indicative of the ubiquitous challenges alliance managers often face in business. The questions themselves are subtle signs of a toxic scarcity, zero-sum mindset pervading most businesses today. In fact, others in the organization would say that an alliance manager's lack of focus on these questions is a sign of personal naïveté at best, or weakness and recklessness at worst. They "logically" say that if we *give* to a relationship we had better *get* back an equal or greater amount. The common belief is that "relationships should be balanced," especially in the financial forms of value.

If we are trying to collaborate in order to create a new technology or expand a market, a competitive mindset shuts down communication and stifles our ability to discover new creative options. It focuses collective attention on value-*extraction*, to the distraction of value-*creation*. This brings a toxic cloud into the alliance, obscuring our collective greatness.

If the first two questions above are inappropriate then, surely the last question, "Are our needs being taken care of?" is worth asking, right? This question does not seem to promote a scarcity-mentality. It can, however, limit perspective. An alliance is about *long-term* value-creation. *Needs* are typically concerned with *near*-term *survival*, not long-term value-creation. There may be times when it *is* necessary to focus on needs, but this has a cost. This near-term focus needs to be time-bound; we need to grow beyond needs. Needy relationships are not very healthy. By focusing on needs alone, we fail to focus on the relationship's true potential for greatness.

As a result of these tensions within our own organizations, we often come face-to-face with *fear*. Others in our organization might fear that we will be taken advantage of by our partner. They might fear that our company's survival is at stake. We have to acknowledge these fears, show how they will be "managed," while not allowing them to sour the climate in our alliance.

Fear becomes more personal as we are questioned, and then we question ourselves, "Are we really doing the right thing for the business?" or "Are we being naïve and weak?" It's worth checking in within ourselves from time to time, and possibly with trusted others, to make sure our motives are clear.

Fear is both cause and effect. Fear causes a scarcity-mentality, and fear is the result of excessive competition. Who or what can we trust in such situations? Ultimately, the answer is trusted others, our Self and the Universe.

Dealing with a lack of trust is hard work. Lack of trust makes alliancing work harder than it needs to be. We have to confront this tough, critically important issue. But how?

Lack of Trust – no foundation

Trust is *the* foundation of relationship.[31]

The level of trust in our alliance directly affects the openness of communication and our ability to discover new value-creating opportunities. In trust-filled relationships we deal with differences and difficulties in a healthy manner. When problems surface we discuss them without negative emotion or blame. We can then *transcend* problems and *transform* them into opportunity. Trust allows us to more deeply collaborate and thus create greater incremental value.

Some in the organization will say that to trust another company is foolish, naïve and dangerous. But healthy trust is incredibly powerful and effective. It is *the* foundation of any alliance. If we cannot trust a partner, the sooner we find that out, the better.

In business relationships where there is a lack of trust, there is a tendency to produce onerous legal agreements. "If we cannot *trust* them, we will *control* them," goes the logic. Contracts are absolutely necessary when dealing with investments and intellectual property (IP) issues; in such areas they are necessary and "good." But they can end up sucking the life out of an alliance. Applied inappropriately, legal contracts can become another "enemy of great."

Legal documents are not the best means for dealing with low-trust. In fact, they can exacerbate the problem when both sides continually refer back to the contract and focus attention on noncompliant behaviors. Beyond their inability to help with trust issues, lengthy detailed contracts cause us to lose sight of the larger value-creating vision now hidden in the midst of legal details.

Also, lengthy contracts stifle the flexibility and adaptability which creativity demands.

We need to use contracts sparingly. Use them to deal with investment, IP issues, governance process, major milestones and deliverables. Use contracts to *help* manage the alliance, but do not let the alliance be managed *by* contracts or the alliance will stagnate and die.

A lack of trust is the primary reason why an alliance fails; it is a sign of an unhealthy alliance. Trust is both cause and effect; therefore, trust is a fundamental issue.

How can we create greater trust in our alliance? The answer seems paradoxical. To create greater trust we must be willing to be lovingly *confrontational*.[32] If we want more trust in an alliance, we must be willing to seek out and embrace situations where greater trust is *needed* or called for, and in that process trust *will grow*; it will come. When we jointly co-front or confront our most difficult problems in a positive and helpful manner, the required trust will be created. As a natural result, trust will come.

Relationship Naïveté – traditional business does not know any better

As experienced alliance managers we know the benefits of investing in relationship.[33] From our personal experience we know that when we improve relationship – internally and externally, interpersonally and between our respective organizations – we will:

- **Negotiate a *better* deal** – as *trust* and *open communication* develop, the parties will discuss, brainstorm and produce more creative, adaptive and effective teaming agreements (legal and non-legal) that enable us to achieve the long-term incremental value both parties expect.

- **Increase the *effectiveness* of the relationship** – with a healthier environment the alliance will deal more positively with change, differences and problems – issues will get surfaced, dealt with and converted into gain.

- **Increase organizational *alignment* and *focus*** – as the atmosphere in the alliance clears up, collective attention focuses on the critical essence in the alliance: (a) a collective vision of incremental *value* and (b) the removal of *impediments* standing in the way of that value.
- **Improve relationship *fit*** – as the organization learns about relationship it can more quickly assess relationship fit with new partners and improve relationship fit with existing partners – this creates a virtuous cycle – as we get better, we get better at being better, which is great.

Given our innate appreciation for relationship, we may, at times, find ourselves at odds with our own organization. In most businesses *relationship* is undervalued. It can be seen by others as "soft," intangible and meaningless stuff. Tough business people may trivialize the relationship topic by describing it as "sitting around the table, holding hands and singing campfire songs." They logically say, "All we need to do is put in place the right business plans, contracts and people, and this relationship stuff will take care of itself. We have more important things to invest in than 'relationship.' So, if our people cannot 'relate,' get new people!"

When managers do start caring about relationship, the topic can be counterintuitive for many of them. Just the phrase "business relationship" looks like two words that do not belong together. Is "business relationship" an oxymoron? What real relationships do we have in business? Aren't they just acquaintances, interactions and exchanges? What *business* is there in relationship? Isn't the business of relationship about romantic match-making, marriage counseling or prostitution?

Relationship in business may be thought of as *unnatural*; but perhaps it is actually the *most natural* and *important* thing going on. By deepening relationship in business things improve, like loyalty. Customer, employee, partner and brand loyalty improve when people feel "a part of," or *in* a relationship. With improved loyalty, businesses improve.

As experienced alliance managers, we understand the subtle art and science of developing value-creating business relationships. From that perspective it can be frustrating when others in the organization want to "help" us. For example, when an alliance is in its early development phase, when we are "negotiating" the deal, a lot of people want to help. This is the visible "sexy" phase of an alliance, when we negotiate agreements and produce joint press releases. But when this highly-visible work is done, the hard work begins, and most of those "helpful" people drift away – leaving us to make it work.

The role of strategic alliance manager is "doing the impossible with nothing" – therefore, we often have to do things that make no sense to others. With insufficient resource, we have to get successful, highly-*competitive* companies to *collaborate*. Our work has to be accomplished through the art of subtle persuasion. Our influence has to pervade into areas of the business beyond our direct control or contact and into another company where we have no direct presence. We need to create trust in low-trust situations. At times we have to go beyond the unnatural, and do things others may "logically" see as naïve, reckless and even dangerous.

- To create *more trust* we have to **be lovingly confrontational**; we proactively embrace situations that require trust in order to get more trust – this seems counterintuitive to others in business. They think trust is something to "earn," but earning trust can take way too long.

- In a problematic alliance, we actually seek out, surface and **openly discuss the biggest problems.** When, "for the sake of the relationship," others want to avoid bringing up problems, they end up creating more problems; avoidance makes things worse, not better.

- To increase our *personal effectiveness* we **give away our best ideas** – we practice **self-obsolescence** in order to increase our personal presence, influence and informal power – hoarding information may have temporary personal gain in other areas of business, but it ends up harming an alliance. We become empowered as we empower others.

Businesses that are serious about alliances but frustrated by their ongoing failure rates may look to traditional business solutions to help. They may bring in strategic consultants, business processes, management systems, metrics and rewards to help "fix" these relationships. These changes can be helpful but are often insufficient for making sustained and meaningful improvement in these strategically-important, long-term business relationships.

At this point management might ask, "What are we missing?"

Could It Be The People? – if so, just tell them, "relate better"

When the implementation of traditional business procedures helps to some degree, but it's not enough, businesses may finally start focusing on *the people* in alliances. Given business relationships occur *between people,* this is an obvious step in the right direction. Businesses benefit as they develop an individual's skills and knowledge in this area, and when they focus on collaborative behaviors. Executives may even issue edicts to "get along better" and "collaborate," accompanied by a list of *behaviors* expected to improve intercompany collaboration.

Successful alliance managers realize the importance of focusing on core issues; deep and bold clarity pays off as we develop our alliance. As our companies take alliancing more seriously and invest in supportive mechanisms, we are encouraged. As the business focuses more on alliance management in skills, knowledge and behavioral training, we feel an acknowledgement of the importance of the role we play in our organization.

Yet, as alliance managers we may still feel somewhat ill-at-ease when we reflect upon what *is* happening and what *is not* happening during these times. We may ask ourselves, "Are the core issues *really* being addressed?" We wonder:

- What acquired knowledge or developed skills will really make a *deep* and long-lasting difference?
- Are we *really* dealing with the *core* issues in relationships and in people?

- Is there an *authentic foundation* from which collaborative behaviors are naturally derived? Can use of this authentic foundation help us make our behaviors more "real" and, hence, more effective?
- What are the *principles* which form the basis for the most effective behaviors?
- If we figure out these *fundamental* principles, can we become adaptive and *predictive* in dealing with a broader range of challenges?

If our organization continues experiencing failure (i.e., mediocre results, lost value-creating opportunities), it may be a sign that we are not getting to the heart the issue. Management may see *some* improvement, but frustration persists as alliance failures continue.

Unconscious-Incompetence – lack of real awareness can lead to harmful results

As our organization invests in strategic alliances, we may see limited or no improvement. Driven by frustration, management's efforts can end up hurting, rather than helping. This is easy to understand when we remember that relationship is not intuitively obvious in most businesses.

As management acknowledges that "people" could be the problem and the solution, they start looking for the right people to manage their strategic alliances. To them the problem may be seen as simply a staffing issue. As Human Resources looks to staff the alliance function with the right people, they may assume all external business relationships are the same. Assuming that is true, then successful sales people can succeed in alliance management. However, there are subtle but significant differences. Sales people *do* work in business relationships; *but* they are focused on value-*exchange,* or more precisely value-*extraction*. And they are driven to close deals as quickly as possible. Asking an individual who has been successful in near-term deal closures to develop *long*-term value-*creating* collaborative relationships is really difficult. It is very hard to change from a near-term "pie-dividing" to a long-term "pie-expanding" mindset. And if these people are successful in their sales jobs, why would they want to change anything about their approach? Typically, from a sales representative's perspective, "alliance people" can be seen as too soft; they are not *driving* their "accounts" hard enough.

Aggressive sales people managing an alliance can easily do more harm than good. A crude description for aggressive sales is to "rape, pillage and burn!" Businesses encourage this behavior with aggressive sales quotas and lucrative commissions. But this type of behavior in a strategic alliance destroys collaborative trust. In an alliance such behavior may get the near-term deal, but with a high long-term cost. They will win the battle but lose the war because, in a healthy alliance, there is no battle.

Overly-aggressive behaviors can also be imposed on us from others in the organization. We may have senior management demand a "win at all cost" or "no-deal is not an option" kind of approach. These individuals honestly believe they are doing the right thing for the business by *making* things happen. But such an attitude can easily over-drive a partner, sour the climate, and result in a sub-optimal deal or no deal at all. We can compare this to an interpersonal relationship. If someone *demands* a dinner date, he may get that date. But it will likely be his last date, and the table chit-chat will surely be strained.

Poor Communication – over-communication is poor communication

Given the complex and risky nature of strategic alliances it is easy for us to over-communicate. We think that maybe if we are completely thorough, the level of risk will diminish. In addition, it may seem necessary to CYA ("cover your ass"), so that when things do blow up, no one can blame us. "I told you, just look at this e-mail!" Given the breadth of an alliance's impact on our organization, we need our communications to be complete. We cannot afford to miss any information that might be important to any of our major stakeholders. We can, therefore, be so completely thorough that key points are lost in painfully-detailed communications.

Given limited resources we have to focus collective attention in order to achieve the alliance's business objectives. Gaining and maintaining alignment is critical to our success. When there is a lack of effective communication, organizational alignment diverges and the alliance fails. We struggle to communicate to all of our stakeholders (constituents) in a useful manner that will maintain organizational alignment. This needs to be done efficiently. We cannot afford to spend all of our personal time custom-communicating to all the different levels and functional areas throughout our organization.

Effective communication, appropriately focused, will help bridge the cultural and strategic chasms that exist in an alliance. Done well, it helps both sides clearly see the incremental value potential and the value-impeding obstacles. Effective communication is a key means by which value-creation occurs.

The question is, "How do we communicate in the midst of so much complexity, when so much is at stake for both companies?" Later we will see that the answer is *clear simplicity*. We simply keep collective attention focused on the incremental value and the removal of value-impediments in the alliance.

Over time, we come to realize that maintaining such simplicity can actually be hard work. And others in the organization may actually have adverse reactions to this simplicity. We will begin to see that just as individuals can be addicted, so can organizations; in this case it's an addiction to complexity.

Organization Addictions to Complexity and Drama – the "yeah, buts ..."

As we get collective attention clearly focused on the simple essence in our alliance, we may start hearing the "yeah, buts" from others:

- "*Yeah, but* it really cannot be that simple.
- "*Yeah, but* what about this important technical or legal detail?"

- "*Yeah, but* what about my favorite program?"
- "*Yeah, but* what about how they treated us last year?"
- "*Yeah, but* what about these dysfunctional personalities or behaviors in their organization?"

It is interesting to sit back and observe this organizational behavior. It is quite astonishing. As we help our alliance clearly see its simple potential and its simple challenges, we start hearing what can only be described as organizational addictive reactions. An addiction is anything we use to avoid facing the truth – to avoid facing the truth within us. Ultimately, we are striving to avoid facing the truth of *who we are*.

In many ways an organization is like a person; it is a body of people. As we focus on the core issues within, on our core challenges, and *especially* on our core greatness, an organization can get nervous. Simplicity brings up nervousness in people because it puts the pressure on them to align and perform. So excuses surface in the form of the "yeah, buts." "Yes, I understand this simple vision and the simple recommendations for overcoming impediments, *but* …"

As individuals we drink, take drugs, shop, work, or have sex to avoid looking within ourselves. When addicts are in recovery, they can start using addictive *behaviors* to avoid facing their greatness. It is common to hear people talk about sabotaging their own success or being their own worst enemy. Alliances can also use addictive behaviors (e.g., complexity and drama) to avoid facing the truth about what's really going on within the alliance and to avoid facing the truthfulness of its own greatness.

We need to see complexity and drama as the organizational "drugs" that they truly are. As people say to newcomers in 12-step recovery who are starting to recover from alcoholism or drug addiction: "There is another way; we don't have to keep living like this." We don't have to keep hiding from our core challenges and hiding from our potential greatness. Complexity and drama are easy things to hide behind. But hiding is not the answer; hiding is actually the problem.

As alliance managers we have to patiently and persistently remind people of the simple essence of our alliance. We have to remind them to focus on creating value and removing value-impediments.

High-Technology, Industry-Specific Challenges – ADHD and proud of it

Each industry has its own collaboration-impeding issues. Below is a discussion of the challenges we face in high-technology alliances (chips, computers, software, etc.) from personal experience. Some of this might be relevant to other industries. Given the increasingly pervasive use of technology, some of this may be applicable to your experiences.

A dominant mantra in high-tech is "change." In 1965, Moore's Law correctly predicted continued exponential growth in computer complexity, doubling every 18-24 months. This ever-accelerating rate of change affects people, organizations, companies, ecosystems and entire industries. Structurally, companies have had to morph from stand-alone solution-delivery entities into active participants in multi-company globally-distributed supply chains. Self-sufficient independence is now global interdependence. Companies realize they cannot do it (solutions) alone. They need each other, now more than ever.

Such a high rate of change, accompanied by high growth, has masked a lot of unhealthy business practices. "Good enough" has sufficed for a long time. With lots of change and growth there seems to be no time to deal with fundamental issues. But cyclical adjustments weed out poor performance. Consider the dot com collapse at the beginning of this century. Afterward, the simplistic use of the word "Internet" was no longer seen as an acceptable indicator of a solid business plan.

There is so much happening each day in high-tech companies that we suffer from organizationally-imposed Attention Deficit Hyperactivity Disorder (ADHD). Given the prevalence of high-tech gadgets, the art of multi-tasking has been taken to new levels. Having a double- or triple-booked calendar is a sign of importance. The new competitive sports in high-tech are competitive calendaring and "black belt" degrees in multi-tasking. But this all comes at a very high cost: loss of *presence* and *shallowness* of thought.

Finally, a highly-competitive and, therefore, anti-collaborative climate is propagated throughout this industry by "successful" ecosystem leaders, like Microsoft and Google. These leaders annihilate or acquire competitors. Increasingly, *fear* seems to be pervading this industry.

Intel's past CEO Andy Grove wrote a very popular business book, *Only the Paranoid Survive*. He wrote, "Sooner or later, something fundamental in your business world will change." Perhaps the time has come for such a fundamental change in how alliances are done – in high-tech and elsewhere. Grove also wrote, "Business success contains the seeds of its own destruction." Perhaps the past success of traditional businesses has itself destroyed healthy alliances and limited sustainable value-creation.

An ever-increasing rate of change in a fear-dominated climate can make alliancing work especially challenging in high-tech.

Summary

Most strategic alliances fail because most businesses fail at "the business of *relationship*."

Most approaches to fix this situation have either been top-down or from-the-outside-in. Management imposes new strategies, systems, procedures, tools or behavioral edicts. Or someone from the outside comes to provide us with the knowledge, skills or behavioral tips that will "fix" things. These changes are helpful but insufficient when dealing with people, relationships and the atmosphere in an alliance.

We are reaching an inflection point when good enough alliancing is no longer acceptable. It is time for greatness.

An inflection point occurs where the old strategic picture dissolves and gives way to the new.
— *Only the Paranoid Survive* by Andy Grove

Spiritual Principles in Strategic Alliances

Focus ...
... where others in the organization cannot / will not focus
_{in the midst}

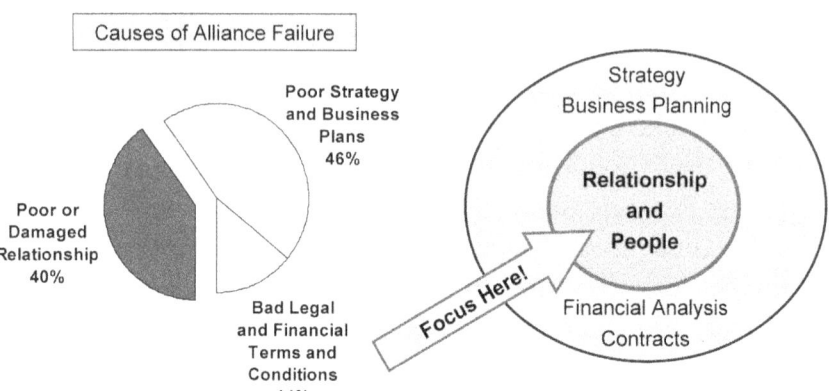

Figure 3.10 – Focus where others need us to focus.

Our greatest problems and our greatest solutions are *between* and, ultimately, *within* people.

It is time to focus on improving attitude & mindset. It is time to focus on the fundamental issues *within*; our **attitude & mindset** directly affects **relationship,** which directly affects the overall **environment** in an alliance. Our personal attitude & mindset is a *causal* factor in our alliance.

Dealing with people and changing attitude & mindset is challenging but richly rewarding work. As alliance managers we intrinsically know that greatness lies in *facing*, not avoiding, our toughest issues. Why should we do anything less than that?

Can we really turn things around?

How can we affect change in core, root cause issues?

How can we fundamentally change and grow?

4. Focus on Personal *AND* Alliance Success (Solution 1 – insights)

First of all, *focus*.

In today's increasingly-complex and highly-competitive world of business, we need to prioritize and we need clear focus. The emergence of strategic alliances as a relatively new form of business relationship is itself evidence of business' need to focus. As alliance managers, we need *laser-sharp focus*. We need to know precisely where we will and will not focus our time and energy in order for us to break through status quo mediocrity and grow into greatness.

For greater personal and organizational success, we must focus.

In Chapter 3 we talked about *why* alliances fail. Figure 3.10 shows us that alliances fail in:

- Legal and financial terms and conditions.
- Strategy and business plans.
- **Relationship.**

To achieve success we must focus on these same areas. The first two areas are *traditional* business practices, which are performed by *others* in the organization. As alliance managers we have to focus on the *nontraditional* causes – relationship & people – where others cannot or will not focus.

The word "people" is added to remind business that relationship occurs between people. We cannot afford to lose sight of the painfully-obvious point that relationship starts with, and ultimately ends within, people. People are the root cause of our problems and the source of our solutions.

Individual success is caused by growth in:

- Knowledge.
- Skills.
- Attitude.

In this section we will start creating a model for alliance management development. A three-by-three table will use areas of personal success as the base framework – **success starts with us**. We will then overlay this framework with the causes of alliance success. The details around the content in this model are open for discussion and healthy debate. Content will vary based on individual alliance managers and their alliances. But the basic three-by-three model is relevant for *all* industries, companies, alliances and alliance managers.

This section concludes with a clear model for how we must prioritize and where we must focus.

Finally, this section explains the many *distractions* we face as we try to prioritize and focus on our most important issues – *attitude & mindset* and *relationship & people*. There are many good and important things that stand between us and our ability to focus on the things which will lead us to greatness; good and important things, like legal, strategy, finance, skills and knowledge. Again, "good is the enemy of great."

Personal Success Factors – the framework

Fifteen years ago, in a professional development course, I heard, "55% of our personal success is determined by our attitude, 30% by the skills we develop and 15% by the knowledge we acquire." Based on life experience these percentages seem to be true. The Society for Human Resource Management verifies these percentages, with an even stronger emphasis on the importance of attitude:[34]

> *Knowledge and skills account for 15% of all the success you will ever enjoy.* **Attitude is far more important** *as it determines* **85%** *of all the success you will ever enjoy.*[35]

In the figure below we have kept the initial conservative percentages, giving knowledge and skills the benefit of doubt. Skills and knowledge are very important in alliancing. We also have added the word "mindset" to "attitude" for a more complete label on this

Focus on Personal AND Alliance Success

most important area of our inner-work. "Attitude" is often used to label behaviors or *external* indicators of what is going on inside. "Mindset" more explicitly focuses us on what is *in* our mind, the central inside stuff. We can fake attitude by *doing* certain behaviors; e.g., we can make ourselves appear confident. When we observe such behaviors in others, they can seem inauthentic. But we cannot fake our own mindset. *We* know what we are thinking inside ourselves. Mindset comes, not from *doing,* but from *being.*

Behavior based on attitude & mindset is authentic. It does not need to be learned, and it is naturally adaptive to any situation.

Focus ...
... on your most challenging and most rewarding cause

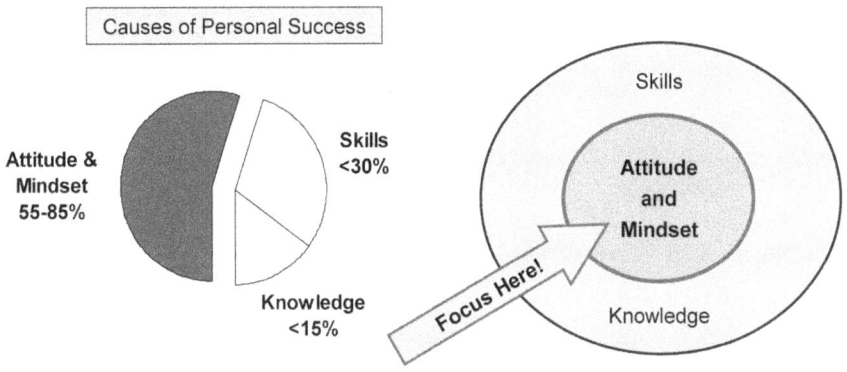

Ref. *The Psychology of Success* by Dobbins, Richard, Pettman, Barrie O from the Society for Human Resource Management. "Knowledge and skills account for 15% of all the success you will ever enjoy. **Attitude** is far more important as it determines **85%** of all the success you will ever enjoy."

Figure 4.1a – Focus on attitude & mindset – our most challenging and rewarding 'cause.'

This framework of knowledge, skills and attitude & mindset illustrates where we as individuals should focus our attention in order to achieve our greatest personal success. Our success is self-

37

determined. We decide what success means for ourselves. For success as a strategic alliance manager, we will now start to populate this personal development framework with content that *causes* alliance success.

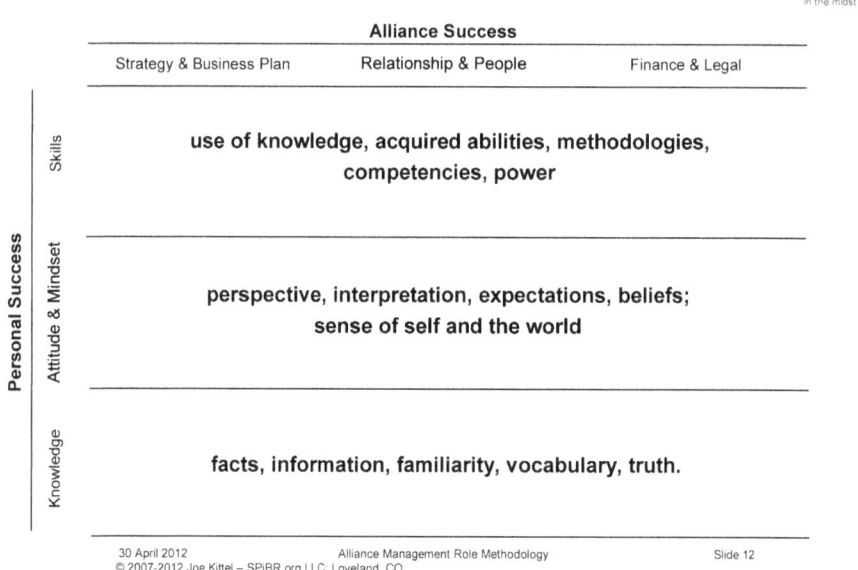

Figure 4.1b – Personal Development – *we* are *the framework* for alliance development.

Alliance Success Factors – bring our substance to bear

The three categories in Figure 3.10 become the columns in a 3x3 table. These are the main areas of work for achieving success in an alliance:

- **Finance and Legal** – causes 14% of alliance failures
    - o This is **visible** work – e.g., negotiating contracts, assessing an alliance and sizing deals.

- It is primarily **the responsibility of others** in traditional areas of an organization: financial planners and lawyers.
  - As alliance managers this *should be* **our secondary focus,** as we help others understand alliancing.
    - We must be able to financially analyze the alliance (especially intangible and long-term forms of value) and manage its formal and informal teaming documents, but we should not allow this important work to completely distract us from our primary focus.

- **Strategy and Business Planning** – causes 46% of alliance failures
  - This is **visible** work – e.g., developing strategic business plans with executives.
  - It is primarily **the responsibility of planners:** corporate, strategic, business and marketing planners in traditional areas of an organization.
  - As alliance managers this *should be* **our secondary focus,** as we help others understand alliancing.
    - The alliance must have a coherent business plan with clear linkages to the plans of the overall business (and plans that develop people and deepen relationship), but we must not allow this work to totally distract us, to the exclusion of our primary focus.

- **Relationship & People** – causes 40% of alliance failures
  - This is often **invisible** and **nontraditional** work – as viewed by many in business, this is often seen as soft, intangible and, therefore, nearly meaningless work.
  - But as alliance managers, this *has to be* **our primary area of focus**; everyone in the alliance will benefit from our focus on relationship.

- If we do not do this work, it will not get done, and our alliances will continue achieving status quo sub-optimal results – we will continue to fail.

- We need to personally focus on **deepening relationship** and creating a healthy **trust-filled climate** for collaboration. We need to enable the discovery of value-creating opportunity. To do this we need to remove value-impediments.

- We need to continually keep the alliance collectively focused on **creating value** and **removing value-impediments**.

The last category listed, "relationship & people," is *the most important thing* for us as alliance managers to work on. But notice how other very important and more visible things can easily stand in the way. We have to deal with these other things in a nontraditional manner. We need to convince others in the business to do the traditional work (planning, finance and legal) in a somewhat nontraditional manner (factoring in relationship and alliancing insights).

We need to "*relationship-ize*" others and "*alliance-ize*" their work:

The **people** who work in the alliance need to become competent in the art and science of **relationship**. They need to understand the importance of relationship and have the necessary skills to span across the intercompany chasm. Finally, they need a positive, collaborative, "can do" attitude & mindset – toward self, others, and both companies.

Critical **work product** done by others needs to incorporate the nuances of **alliancing**. Strategic plans, financial analysis work and teaming documents (including legal contracts) need to reflect and account for the subtle nuances of alliancing work, such as intangible forms of value, long-term perspectives, risk taking, vision and relationship development.

Here are some initial and unique thoughts on the alliance-specific substance of our personal work. Later in this chapter, suggested details of this substance will be used to populate the development framework introduced in Figure 4.1b.

Financial and Legal

When we talk with others about our alliance we often primarily focus on the financials: each company's corporate revenue, investments in the alliance, and alliance-leveraged sales revenue. This natural tendency distracts us in two ways. First, a sole focus on financial value distracts us from intangible forms of value. An alliance's intangible forms of value often *exceed* tangible forms. If you cannot accept this concept as true, can you accept that it is the invisible or intangible things that lead to the tangible?

Second, by solely focusing on revenue we can get distracted from where we personally need to focus – relationship & people. We do need to make sure that the financial work is done well, but despite its attraction, this is *not* our primary area of focus. As relationship improves, the alliance's financial performance will improve. Finance performance will take care of itself if the alliance is healthy. This is analogous to romantic relationships; if there is love in the relationship, the birth of children will naturally take care of itself. This is not to say that we should completely ignore the financials, but that we should come from a place that is grounded in people and relationship.

Legal and contractual issues are seductively visible areas of work. Even though this area accounts for only 14% of alliance failures, it can be where we invest a disproportionate amount of our time. It sounds impressive to tell someone, "I am 'negotiating.'" Few people have the opportunity to directly participate in intercompany negotiations. When we are in active negotiations, our work appears mystical. People around us might say, "Don't bother him now; he's 'negotiating!'" And we can make ourselves appear very important as we relay to others the challenges we face with the partner, with our own attorneys and with the nuanced complexity of important legal issues (e.g., intellectual property, indemnification or residual rights). Our primary role in negotiations is to ensure that:

- We collectively **do not lose sight of the end-point** value-creating *vision*; that we do not lose sight of the big issues in the midst of legal jargon and contractual details.

- The overall **atmosphere stays positive,** pie-*expanding* and value-*creating*. Even though we are negotiating we need to assure that within the alliance we are *collaborating*, not competing.

- **Important issues get addressed** and not ignored or avoided; that we have healthy, open and unemotional *confrontation* in order to surface and resolve important issues. We need to not have interpersonal conflict.

- Interpersonal and intercompany **relationships deepen and improve** during the negotiations. More than simply not *damaging* relationships we can use these periods of intense discussion to actually *deepen* relationships.

Strategy and Business Planning

Like the "negotiate" word, "strategic" and "alliance" are also seductively important words. Our work sounds impressive when we say, "I manage a 'strategic alliance.'" Sometimes we may try to hide behind "strategic" when someone asks us how the corporation has *really* benefited from our alliance. In response we might say, "This relationship is 'strategic.'" This conveys the idea that, "This alliance is too complex for your simple mind to grasp." Most importantly, "Don't bother me with these questions. I am too busy. *I* am 'strategic.'"

We do need to know that our company's strategic business plans are solid and that the alliance's supportive role is clear. In the area of strategic business planning, we and our alliance should play a strong supportive role. Corporate business strategy should drive the alliance; the alliance should *not* drive the business – it should influence it, but not drive it. As is true in contractual work, we need to make sure that collective attention stays focused on the right things, at the right time, and in the right manner. Everyone involved in the alliance needs to stay focused on its core essence, the vision for incremental value, and removal of value-impediments. This collective attention is best achieved via an inclusive collaborative manner.

Finally, in the business' plans we need to make sure that we are *investing* in *relationship*. Relationship *is* a major root cause of failure or success and, therefore, must be accounted for in the strategic plans. The business needs to view its ability to develop relationship as a strategic asset. There should be performance metrics to make us personally accountable for relationship improvement results.[36]

Relationship & People

This *is* our **primary** area of focus; 40% of our alliance's success rests on how well people in the alliance relate.

We need to help others who work in the alliance develop their own understanding of and competency in relationship work. No one else can or will focus on relationship & people in the manner needed to achieve the true potential of our alliance. If we don't do relationship work, it will not get done, and the alliance will fail (stay stuck in mediocre performance). That is how important *we* are to the business. It is for this purpose that this book is written – to help get you more focused on the most important issue in strategic alliance management – *relationship & people*.

Now we start populating our personal development framework with content tied to alliance success. We will start with the *least* important area (knowledge) and conclude with the *most* important area (attitude & mindset). The reason for this least-to-most-important structure is to illustrate how easy it is for us to be distracted from focusing on our most important issues. We see how very important things can easily stand in the way of great things; how "good *is* the enemy of great."

Knowledge – affects <15% of personal success

Knowledge: familiarity, vocabulary, facts, information, truth.

In general, knowledge is the *easiest* thing to assess and the easiest thing to change. But as compared to the other two areas, acquired knowledge has the *least* impact on our success. It is interesting, therefore, that knowledge is often the thing *most* focused on. For example, in hiring interviews we often hear, "So, what do you *know* about __[*fill in the blank*]__?"

As we start to become familiar with a new job, we begin using the right jargon, often without knowing what the words really mean. We are able to spew forth lots of facts and sound impressive. In alliancing we are expected to possess nearly endless knowledge about our partner. It *is* reasonable for others to expect us to be the *most all-knowing* person about our alliance. But we cannot know everything. It is important for us to focus on knowing what is important and somewhat ignore the less important.

"Truth," the last synonym listed above, takes knowledge to a different level. When we come to *know* the *truth* about someone or something, we actually become empowered. The power of knowing the truth, especially as it relates to who we are and what's going on within us and between us, *is* the purpose of this book. In a spiritual sense this truth of who we are overlaps with attitude & mindset. Our proximity to this core truth affects our *perspective*, which is a primary attribute of attitude & mindset. But … "truth be known" … we digress … let's get back to knowledge.

What do we need to know in order to be successful? Below are some examples of important areas of personal knowledge that are critical for alliance success. This list is neither complete nor representative of all companies and all industries. This list is intended to illustrate how very important things distract us from the alliance's need for us to focus on *relationship & people*. We can easily allow good things to distract us from great things. As you can see, to attempt to know everything included in the list would be too much for any one person, hence, the need for us to prioritize and focus.

Financial and Legal

- **Major terms used in financial analysis.** Know what good financial analysis looks like so that the alliance's investments are based on a solid foundation. Understand things like income, revenue, profit, NPV, break-even-time, investment, ROI, loss, assets, liability, etc.

- **Key legal issues, terms and conditions.** Critical legal issues like indemnification, intellectual property rights, confidentiality, limitation of liability, residual rights, company policy on exclusivity or time-to-market advantage, personnel non-recruit clauses, etc. We need to know these issues well enough so that we can grow our alliance while protecting our company.

- **Regulatory issues.** Regulatory issues: anti-trust or noncompetitive behaviors, Sarbanes-Oxley, monopolistic issues, industry-specific regulations, ethics and transparency, etc.

- **Use of formal vs. informal agreements.** What is appropriate to put into a formal, legally-binding contract versus an informal, ever-changing teaming document? When, where and why do we use one form rather than the other? What are the tradeoffs?

Strategy and Business Planning

- **Recognize a good business plan.** Know what a good strategic business plan looks like. Know how these plans will **address relationship & people** development in the alliance.

- **Understand both companies.** Know both companies' strategy, organization, decision-making processes, customers, competitors, business ecosystems, products, services and technologies. Know the other side better than they know themselves.

- **Know the trends.** Understand key trends in globalization, industry, ecosystem, competitive landscape, customers, technologies, technical interconnectedness, regulations, etc.

- **Understand the linkages between alliance and corporate.** Know how the alliance is contributing to corporate success, near-term and long-term, and vice versa. Have a clear, strong alliance plan. Know how the corporation will make use of the value the alliance produces. Recognize when the organization strongly or weakly supports the alliance's plans.

Relationship & People

- **Know yourself; be true to yourself.** Relationship starts with you and from within you. Your external relationships start with your internal relationship with your Self. Who do you think you are?

- **Know both companies.** Get a clear understanding of relationship & people issues – especially around intercompany cultural and strategic differences. Know the organizational structures and decision-making processes of both companies. Understand the people you work with – in order to connect, empathize and relate.

- **Sources of power and influence.** Know the true source of your power and influence. Know that power comes from giving away what we know, by *giving away our ideas*. Know that this giving-of-self is naturally reciprocated by others and then *extends our presence* throughout the alliance.

As we scan down this list we see lots of important things that we do need to know. Where do we start? From the business' perspective we need to *start* with relationship & people. Relationship & people issues rarely improve with avoidance; over time they get worse, not better. Again, no one else in the organization can or will focus on these things. We need to stay focused there. That is the best thing we can do for all concerned.

Focus on Personal AND Alliance Success

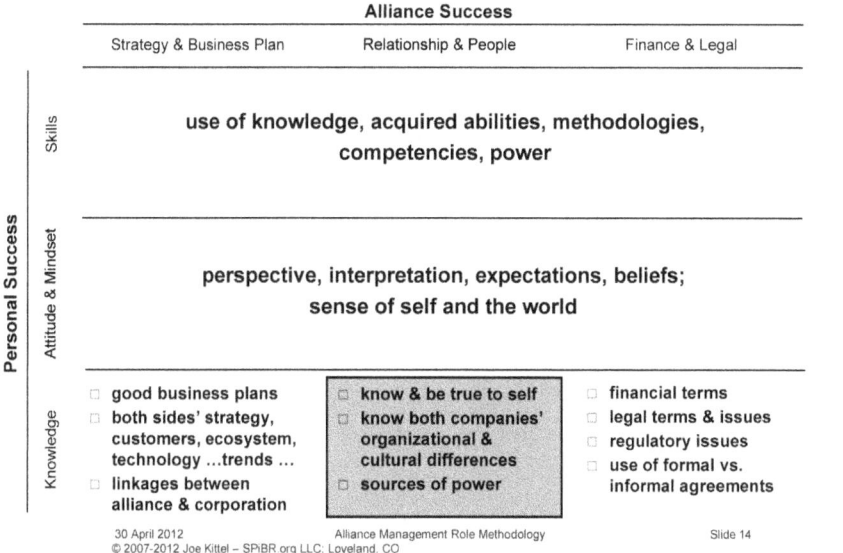

Figure 4.3 – Knowledge – facts, information, familiarity, vocabulary, truth.

Skills – affects <30% of personal success

Skills: the *use* of knowledge, acquired abilities, methodologies, competencies (often without insight), learned power (often without understanding the source of that power)

In terms of impact, skills lie between knowledge, and attitude & mindset. Compared to knowledge, skills are harder to assess and harder to develop. But it is easier to develop skills than to change attitude & mindset.

We grow in personal effectiveness and become more empowered as we develop our skills. We are better at our work. But we may not have a clear understanding as to the fundamental principles at play. We can solve problems and make things better. But we are not quite sure *why* these skills work. We grow in our ability to impact situations and people. But we may not understand the source

47

of that power. Empowerment of self and others can, therefore, become a hit-and-miss game. We do become more competent. But we may end up being locked into a specific set of scenarios where we can apply our skills. But if something unforeseen comes up, we might not know what to do.

Required alliance management skills will vary based on industry, company, maturity of the alliance and alliance type. Focusing too much on skills can distract us from focusing on attitude & mindset issues. These things are very important, but they can still be distractions from where we really need to focus. We need to enable others in the organization to do many of these tasks, rather than do all of them ourselves. Only then can we focus our attention where the business needs us to focus – on deepening relationship. Below is a list of skills helpful in alliancing (this is not necessarily a complete list):

Financial and Legal

- **The ability to translate intangible value into tangible value.** The capacity to develop and use organizationally-acceptable financial (or tangible) metrics that can represent the value-enabling *intangible* or invisible forms of value. The ability to do reasonably detailed financial analysis. To analyze an alliance's performance, collectively and for individual programs. Visible value is first conceived in the invisible.

- **Capability to "Alliance-ize" lawyers and financial folk.** The ability to help others "get it" in terms of the core essence in your alliance – value and impediments. To help lawyers be more *open and risk-tolerant*. To help the people in finance to accept *intangible value as meaningful*. Also, to help both lawyers and finance be more patient.

- **The ability to help others value relationship.** The capability to help management and the broader organization appreciate the strategic value of *relationship*. The ability to develop and protect relationships in the world of business.

- **Capacity to develop and use informal teaming documents.** The ability to create non-binding teaming documents. The *evolutionary use* of these tools to continually *refocus collective attention* on the core issues. To do this in an adaptive and flexible manner. Facilitating the ongoing discovery and evolutionary development of your alliance's value-creating vision.

- **Use of formal legal contracts.** From an alliancing perspective, contracts should be used primarily for such things as intellectual property issues, significant investments, major deliverables, governance processes, and escalation procedures. Things that are strategically important in the alliance and that can *tolerate* being "locked" into a legal contract. Simply amending a contract is often a contentious process, which an alliance should not get exposed to, except when absolutely necessary.

Strategy and Business Planning

- **The ability to conduct tactful due diligence assessments of a partner and of one's own company.** Skills to tactfully, yet thoroughly, assess strategic, cultural, organizational and technical competencies. Assess in a thorough, respectful and appreciative manner.

- **Capability to establish clear strategic linkages between the corporation and the alliance.** The ability to evaluate strategic business plans and marketing plans. To see how a partner can contribute to and positively influence those plans. To see unforeseen opportunities and challenges.

- **The ability to develop and implement alliance plans.** The knack to develop a clear and compelling vision of where the alliance is going. The ability to "message" this vision to the corporation, your partner, customers, industry analysts and the broader ecosystem (even to competitors). The capacity to establish and maintain strong organizational alignment within each company and across the alliance interface. Organizational time management skills – to keep everyone focused on the right thing, in the right place and at the right time. The ability to ignore what should be ignored. The efficient use of the organization's systems and processes for managing the traditional business and alliances.

- **The capacity to "alliance-ize" strategic business planners.** Getting relationship issues, with performance metrics, incorporated into plans. To have relationship be seen as an integral part of strategic business plans and managed as a corporate asset. Expand perspectives on value. Increase organizational patience and persistence.

Relationship & People

- **Management of self.** Personal time management skills. Clearly and confidently know what should and should not be done at any point in time. It has been said that if you cannot say "no" to what you shouldn't do, you cannot say "yes" to breakthrough priorities. Prioritize and focus, and then define the next right step.

- **The ability to listen holistically.** To deeply listen to others and the organization. The capability to *hear what the alliance is saying*. "In the midst," hear of its potential and its challenges. To assertively and openly listen one-on-one. To allow others to speak of the unspeakable in empathetic and trust-filled settings. To hear what is *not* said. To accept and embrace differences. To coalesce individual perspectives into a collective whole. Listen again, *continually listen, deeply listen …*

- **Accept then embrace differences.** The capacity to have open, *loving confrontation*. To jointly face our most difficult challenges in the alliance without emotion, blame or guilt. To accept and transcend, then embrace and transform differences.

- **Use of nontraditional "relationship-izing" skills.** The capacity to confidently perform nontraditional practices that enable greater value-creation:[37]
    o   the power in simplicity

- o   presence and rapport building
- o   awareness and holistic listening
- o   being lovingly confrontational in order to build trust
- o   focusing collective attention
- o   spiritually-based negotiating
- o   self-obsolescence
- o   being an illuminating mirror
- o   creating a productive community
- o   using relationship as a strategic asset

Then conduct just-enough and just-in-time training throughout the alliance. Unobtrusively help others use these nontraditional skills to achieve greater business and personal success.

- **The ability to help others quickly "get it."** Help those who work in your alliance understand what it is about and how to effectively engage with the partner. How to work with each other. How to overcome obstacles. Then communicate this in whatever means is necessary: one-on-one, meetings, e-mails, presentations, teaming documents, legal contracts and strategic plans.

Again, we might scan back through these three lists, not looking for incompleteness or errors, but looking at how hard it is for us to get to the critically important area of relationship & people. No wonder so many alliances fail. We may be unconsciously enabling them to fail by working on important matters, and avoiding the *most* important matters.

Alliance managers are sometimes either unable or unwilling to get to the relationship & people stuff. Sometimes the organization does not allow us to delve into it. There are so many other, urgent, important and visible things that we can work on; it is hard for us to find the time to work on relationship & people.

We can easily let important matters stand in the way of what truly matters.

Skills
use of knowledge, abilities, methodologies, competencies

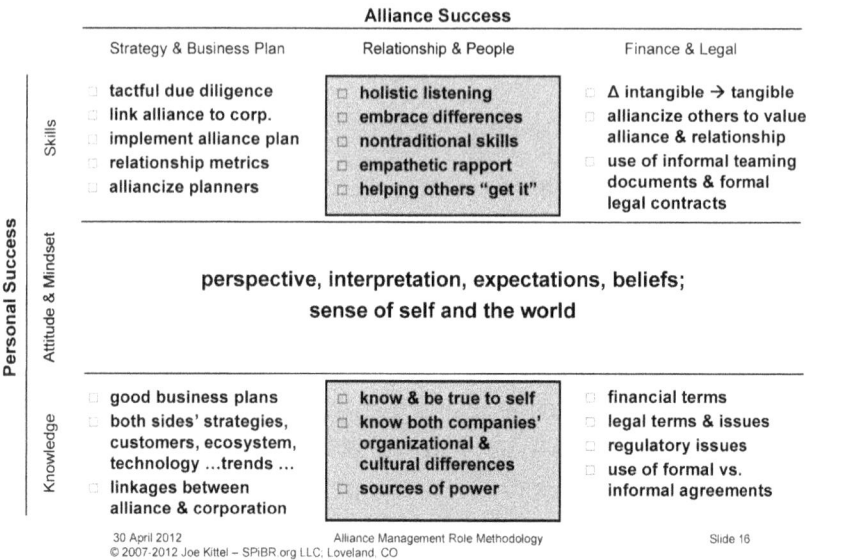

Figure 4.4 – Skills – use of knowledge, abilities, methodologies, competencies.

Attitude & Mindset – affects 55-85% of personal success

Attitude & mindset: our *chosen perspective* of others and events, our interpretation of events, and expectations (especially of the future). Attitude & mindset are grounded in deeply-held beliefs and values originating from our core sense of Self and our sense of the world around us.

The words "attitude" and "mindset" really need to be used together because, when combined, they are complete in concept and more effective in action. Analyzed separately, we see how they form parts of a powerful whole. Attitude is often about someone's disposition and the way a person views something or tends to behave toward it. One's attitude may be happy, confident or positive; one may view others through a positive or negative lens. Mindset, however, is more explicitly about what is going on *in* the mind, the thoughts we consciously choose and the frame of mind we hold. Attitude tends to be more about *behavior*, whereas mindset tends to be more about what's happening *within*. One may have a scarcity or abundance mindset, for example, which in time will affect that person's behavior. In terms of effectiveness and success in alliancing, attitude can't be addressed without examining mindset, and vice versa. For this reason, I combine them as "attitude & mindset" as a reminder of their interconnectedness and importance.

Attitude & mindset are the most difficult factors to assess and change. Common belief is that it is nearly impossible to change someone's attitude & mindset; that these things are innate; that we are born with them or that they are deeply rooted in our earliest childhood. "Attitude & mindset are fixed," is common thinking. Given this assumption, the best we can hope to do is to accurately *assess* it. At least then we can hire the right people.

However, the belief that "we cannot change attitude & mindset" is flawed thinking. It says that, at our core, we incapable of any real personal growth. This denies the positive impact of life's experiences. Life compels us all to grow – people, organizations, companies, countries and humanity. We either grow or die – but not necessarily physically. Life events, or the universal force of love, compel us all to grow. If we choose to believe we cannot grow, we live miserable lives. We end up fighting life, others and most importantly ourselves. If we accept the idea that growth is associated with love, a world without growth is loveless. Our other choice is to accept and embrace growth, starting within. Acceptance is the starting point; embracement comes later.

How can we begin? We can start by hiring the right people; behavioral interviewing *can* help toward that end. But behavior alone can be a misleading indicator of attitude & mindset. Someone may be *doing* the right things, but they are not quite sure *why* those things work. For example, in interpersonal communications we may have been taught to paraphrase what another person said and to repeat it back so they know that you heard them. Some people may get stuck in mindlessly repeating back what others say, either verbatim or paraphrased. When we observe this we sense a lack of integrity or that they are not being genuine. Such ungrounded or inauthentic behavior can do more harm than good. On the other hand, when behavior is naturally derived from attitude & mindset, it is more authentic, and it doesn't requires us to memorize how we should behave in specific situations.

A key result from a change in attitude & mindset is to make behavior natural and authentic. Healthy attitude & mindset allow us to be more adaptive and flexible. This enables us to deal positively with any situation. Attitude & mindset are *fundamental principles* in people, and in relationships they:

- Help us understand *why* specific alliancing skills work – enlightening us as to their "mechanics."
- Coalesce prior experiences, taking us to a higher level of understanding.
- Enable a broadened range of problem-solving – empowering and inspiring, leading to creativity.
- Possess a certain predictive nature, allowing our longer-term vision to be clearer.
- Help us know what knowledge is important and *why*.

Such are the business and personal benefits of going deeply within self to change attitude & mindset.

Financial and Legal

- **Respect for lawyers and financial analysts**. Treat financial and legal personnel with utmost respect. Be patient as they become sensitized to the nuances of alliancing. Willingly listen and learn from them and with them.
- **Perceive legal work as protecting the overall business.** See legal work as necessary for the protection of the overall business. Legal contracts protect a company's intellectual, financial and human assets.
- **Perceive financial work as providing the business' lifeblood.**

In many ways finance runs a business and, therefore, it runs your alliance. If we cannot address the financial needs of the business, there will be no business. If your alliance cannot justify its existence based ultimately on its financial value to the business, *it* should not exist. This is why it is so important to translate long-term and intangible forms of value into forms of value that are acceptable in a business' financial analysis; this is hard work, but it is strategically important.

- **Be patient and persistent.** It is reasonable to expect the broader organization to provide supportive financial and legal services to your alliance. But remember, these are traditional business processes and the people there are often traditionally-minded. It is likely that they have had little experience in alliancing. Our role is to help them understand the *nontraditional* aspects of alliancing so we can all be more focused and effective. We help them confront risk, see longer-term and expand their ideas around value.

Strategy and Business Planning

- **Be collaborative with planners.** We treat individuals involved in strategic business planning with utmost respect. We are patient as they become sensitized to the nuances of alliancing. We are willing to listen and learn from them and with them, establishing healthy relations that maintain the alliance's strategic business planning "tentacles" to the corporation.

- **Perceive strategic business plans as vision.** We see planning activities as establishing an intelligent *vision* for the business. They provide direction for achieving our future growth.

- **Realize strategic business plans provide contextual meaning.** Your alliance's connections to these plans are the "tentacles" that gives the alliance *meaning* and *purpose*.

- **See the alliance as *part of* the overall business.** Your alliance needs to show how it supports a business' strategic business plans. Insights gained from the alliance are fed back into and positively influence those plans. The alliance demonstrates that it is *part of* the overall business.

- **See and share unique perspectives**. Your alliance has its own strategic plan. This plan addresses *nontraditional* processes, *intangible* values and *long*-term perspectives. It is focused on the core issues in the alliance. Such perspectives are broadly shared and understood by others in the business.

Relationship & People

Encouraging us to primarily work at the intersection of (a) relationship & people and (b) attitude & mindset *is* the purpose of this book. The ideas shared below are neither definitive nor absolute. They are shared to stir up thinking. Such is the purpose of the 3x3 table, Figure 4.6 – to stir up thinking and bold focus us on the most important core issues, not necessarily on the details.

- **Be enthused by challenge, knowing challenge brings growth.** We realize that great insight lies on the other side of challenge. When problems surface, we confront them immediately and in a healthy, open manner. Differences present opportunity to first accept and transcend, later embrace and transform. Differences are not to be avoided, neutralized or managed, but are to be used, like the lead and acid in a car battery.

- **Perceive others as self**. Start with a strong sense of Self. We are true to Self and true to others. Perceive "we" or oneness, not "us vs. them." We are focused on the oneness of us all. We see the alliance as a strong cohesive team, trying to do what is right. Problems and answers lie between us, in the midst; within that in-betwixt chasm is the magic.

- **Hold a timelessness of perspective and presence.** We are clearly in the here and now. We embrace a unique perspective of time. We see the interconnectedness of events and trends. We connect the dots – we complete the picture across time and space. Do not bring up "bad" events from the past.

We are fully present, fully engaged, always and everywhere. Timelessness leads to patience. We avoid living the lie of multi-tasking. We are focused.

- **Be mindful, thoughtful and creative.** We realize the immense creative power of thought. We see the big picture, things others choose not to see. We are a strategic future-looking thinker, grounded in today's reality. As pragmatic visionaries we are comfortable being "where the rubber meets the blue sky." We are open-minded, willing to accept and embrace another's reality as his truth.

- **Focus on goodness.** We choose to see the good in all. We see only the good in others and in situations – not with blinders on, but by *overlooking* or *looking past* the bad. We are positive, optimistic and focused on solution. We possess a positive outlook on the future of any given situation. We know deep within that the right thing for all will eventually come to pass. Greatness is simply a matter of time.

Changes in attitude & mindset authentically affect other things. Attitude & mindset are *causal* in its nature; attitude & mindset affect positive behavioral changes like:

- Personal confidence – good eye contact.
- Courageous aloneness – a willingness and boldness to stand alone and promote unpopular decisions.
- Empathetic connectedness – ability to build rapport. Able to say, "I don't know" and "I was wrong."
- A sense of gratitude – toward self and others – egoless – a powerful team player and leader.
- Attentive- and assertive-listening – to others, to the collective organization.
- Trust – high-ethics and transparency. Naturally grounded in oneness and integrity.
- Persistence and tenacity – willingness to go wherever, talk with whomever, and do whatever is necessary.

- Tough on tasks, but soft on people – assertiveness coupled with niceness.

The usefulness of specific attitudes & mindsets vary based on industry, company, and the development phase or type of alliance. Pharmaceutical alliances often call for more control and risk-avoidance than high-technology. During exploratory trailblazing and opportunity-discovery we need to have a different mindset than in the turn-the-crank phase. A co-development alliance calls for different attitudes than a market-making alliance.

The Insightful Intersect – Relationship & People | Attitude & Mindset

The following table summarizes the intersect points between specific causes of personal success *and* causes of alliance success.

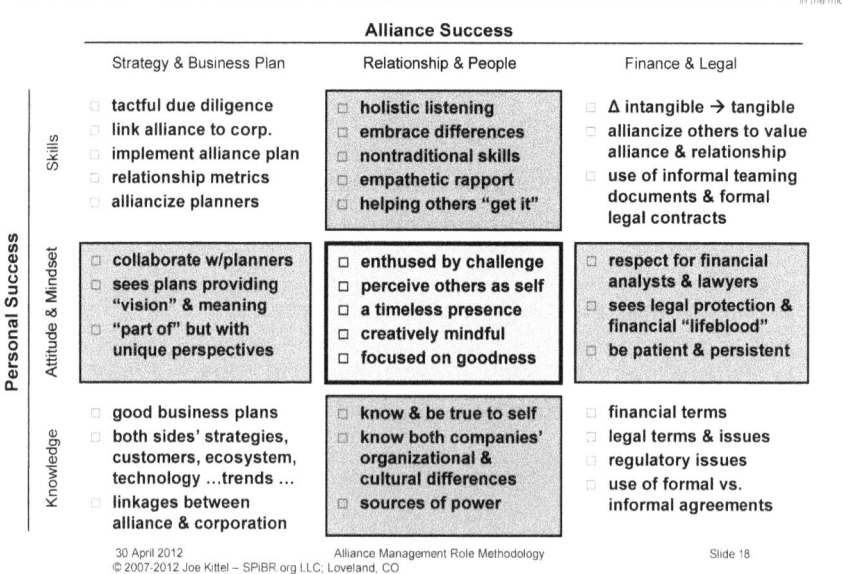

Figure 4.6 – Focus: (1) on the core issues in self, *and*
(2) on the nontraditional issues in the alliance.

So far this chapter has been complex. We have been exploring and then integrating personal development with alliance success. Complexity, thus far, is understandable, or at least to be expected. But it is now time to simplify. We are striving for the simplicity that lies on the other side of complexity; not simplistic naiveté, but wise simplicity – simplicity coupled with experience-based wisdom is our objective.

Simply speaking:

- *We have **one** primary focus.* We should always be about **changing attitude & mindset** (our own and other's) in order to **improve and deepen relationships** throughout our alliance.

We are the leader of the alliance. If we do not do this, who will? Is there anything more important for us to be working on? From time to time there may momentarily be more urgent things, but *nothing more important*.

- **We have two secondary foci.**
  - o **Relationship & People**. Here we must lead by example – we must ***be* the change**.

    We help those who work directly in the alliance, through **just-enough, just-in-time training**. We help them improve their knowledge, skills, attitude & mindset in the area of business relationships and their working relationships with others.

    We need to **"relationship-ize"** the *people* who are working *in* our alliance.

  - o **Attitude & Mindset**. Especially in this area we have to ***be* the change**.

    We bring our collaborative mindset everywhere we go. We have to positively impact the strategic planning, finance and legal processes. We need to help the people who do this work understand alliancing. They may not personally need to improve their own relationship competencies, but the things they produce (e.g., documents and processes) need to be "alliance-ized." Plans, contracts and teaming agreements need to incorporate alliancing ideas. They need to embrace the ambiguities inherent in alliances, such concepts as risk, change, uncertainty, relationship metrics, intangible value and long-term returns.

We need to **"alliance-ize" the *work*** of the people who are working *for* our alliance.

- **"Other."** Time permitting, or as needed, we might get into some of the details of traditional business practices like strategic planning, finance or contracts. It might be good to deepen our understanding in these areas. We do need a working knowledge, especially of key issues. But remember, these things really should be done by someone else.

Negotiating skills are critically useful for us and directly relevant throughout the practice of alliancing. We are, after all, *always* negotiating – we are always having *substantive discussion*. But negotiating is relevant far beyond contractual work. In any alliance, the most effective negotiating is grounded in holistic listening, embracing differences, and creative brainstorming.[38] Principles and practices discussed in Chapters 6 and 8 will deepen relationship and complement negotiating processes. Negotiating training, especially the *Program on Negotiation* at Harvard, MIT and Tufts Universities is very helpful and highly-recommended.[39]

Insights gained in the process as summarized in Figure 4.6 (the 3x3 matrix) will come from the deepening of *relationship* between the alliance *manager* and alliance *management*. Useful ideas will come out by examining the overlap or relationship between personal development and alliance development; this is a different perspective on relationship, this is about the relationship between *ideas*. This section is about closely looking at the relationship between a person and his job. As a result we will gain a new perspective, greater insight and increased organizational alignment. This illustrates a powerful concept in relationship work:

*Answers always lie **in the midst** – in the between.*

Summary

So, this chapter boils down to this. As strategic alliance managers we have a simple core focus:[40]

Improve attitude & mindset in order to deepen relationship.

In time this focus will lead to increased value-creation. This sounds simple, but it is *not easy*. This is hard work, requiring confidence and persistence. But this can be very fulfilling work.

Secondarily, we help others. We provide service. We help others understand how to *relate* better. We do this first by our own example, more precisely by *being*. Throughout the process we use just-in-time, just-enough and often unseen-by-others teaching opportunities. We help those who are *doing* the work for our alliance better understand the nature of alliancing. This is especially important in the areas of strategic business plans, financial analysis and legal contracts.

Explicit *non*-focus areas are the actual work of financial analysis, strategic planning, contracts, marketing and sales. We must have a working knowledge and some skills in these critically important areas. There may be times when we have to go deep into specific topics or important activities. But through the art of subtle persuasion we should attract others to do the actual work – for us and for our alliance. This traditional business work needs to be done in a manner conducive to long-term collaborative value-creation.

The people *in* the alliance need to be relationship-ized. The people working *for* the alliance need to have their work alliance-ized.

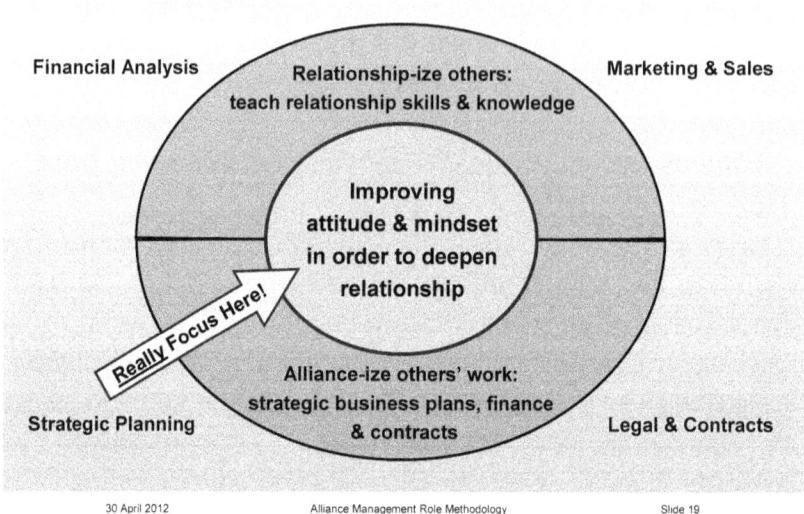

Figure 4.7 – Our Foci.

We focus, focus and focus in order to achieve greater success, be more effective and "have more fun than one person deserves." This degree of focus brings with it attractive integrity and informal power. Being of meaningful service to others brings us joy. We will grow to love our work and work our love.

> *Work is love made visible. And if you cannot work with love but only with distaste, it is better that you should leave your work and sit at the gate of the temple and take alms of those who work with joy.*
>
> — *The Prophet* by Kahlil Gibran

5. Role Clarity – who am I? (Problem or Solution)

So far in this book we have described the difficulties, complexities and trends in strategic alliances. We have discussed the paradoxical trend that alliances are *growing* in importance and use, while *continuing to fail* to achieve their expected results. This trend cannot continue. We cannot keep living like this.

We have looked at the causes of alliance failure with appropriate emphasis on the nontraditional area of relationship. We then looked at where success must come from – the intersection of personal attitude & mindset with relationship & people.

Looking boldly at this intersection we have gained insights around our primary and secondary foci. We should primarily focus on changing attitude & mindset in order to deepen and improve relationship. Secondarily, we should focus on relationship-izing people and alliance-izing their work.

As we now look at our role, our job description, it is worth remembering that this book is written **by and for alliance managers** – those doing this work.[41]

Here are a few questions to assess the value of this section. Does this section help us:

- **Fundamentally change** how we think about ourselves and our job, so we can start reversing the abysmal failure rates of alliances?

- See the various forms of distraction so we can better **focus** in the midst of daunting difficulty and overwhelming complexity? See how admittedly important and good things can stand between us and greatness?

- Start seeing how we might more effectively uncover and create incremental **value** by *being* the required change?

Lack of Role Clarity Adversely Affects Success Rate

It is dangerous to make assumptions, especially when it affects our job. But in today's fast-paced world of business we have to make some assumptions. So, as alliance managers, we assume we know what our job is about. Management assumes that we know, too. And we both assume our views align.

In this section we will explore the role of strategic alliance manager. We will see how there can often be significant lack of clarity and misalignment between the alliance manager and others in the organization. Our primary point of view is the alliance manager's perspective. This section boldly explores our most important question:

Who do I think I am?

After answering this question, management can then consider their perspective on our job. Who do *they* think we are? Who do we both think alliance managers *should* think they are?

After we have defined our job and aligned with management, only *then* can we work with management to collaboratively answer such questions as:

- How can we be more effective? Where should we focus our limited attention, time, energy and resource?
- How can we increase our level of job satisfaction? How can we have more fun at work? Can we?
- How can management help us be more effective in our job?
- How will we know when our job is done?
- When is a specific task really someone else's job?
- How should we define success – personally and for our alliance?
- What should our job performance metrics be? What should they not be?[42]

Role Clarity – who am I?

This chapter shows how the obscurity of our own job description can be one of our greatest obstacles, adversely affecting us, the alliance and business. The early parts of the chapter looked at problems and challenges. Later we will get into solution with some bold and thought-provoking questions and suggestions.

Specific details vary based on industry and company. But in-depth exploration of role will be helpful for any alliance manager. The result will be increased alignment with management and the organization.

A Singularly Unique Job

The role of strategic alliance manager is unique, complex and ambiguous. Uniqueness and complexity are derived from an alliance's impact on *every* functional area of business (e.g., strategy, legal, research and development, finance, marketing and sales).

Ambiguity can easily enter in when this role is viewed from the frame of reference of an individual's prior work experience. For example, someone coming from sales may view this job as account management. Ambiguity also comes from the nontraditional nature of the alliance manager job. Alliance management does not fit neatly into traditional organizational roles, like marketing, sales or procurement. Our management can struggle to decide where we should reside in the organization. Should our role be centralized or distributed out? At what level of the organization?

As alliance managers, we have to play a broad range of roles: executive liaison, negotiator, "good cop" *and* "bad cop," the relationship guy, task-master, escalation fixer, cheerleader, spokesperson, etc. This makes our job seem ambiguous and ill-defined. When others in the organization cannot easily understand a role in the organization, they often treat it as unimportant, the logic being, "If a job cannot be simply described, its value to the organization must be low. Therefore, people doing that work can be ignored."

As a starting point in our discussion here, and as a reference point for later on, it is both insightful and empowering to realized that strategic alliance managers:

Do the impossible – with nothing – in the eye of a hurricane.

"Do the *impossible* …" – Our job entails getting two highly-*competitive* companies, in a predominantly fear-based climate, to *collaborate*. Each company is rightly focused on competing and winning. In such a setting collaboration is very unnatural. Changing the environment in an alliance from competitive to collaborative, changing thoughts from being fear-based to openly trustful, is nearly impossible. We also have to span our company's entire business while simultaneously straddling the cultural and strategic chasms between the two companies. This seems to be impossible, too. The current failure rate in alliancing supports this impossibility argument.

"… *with nothing* …" – We rarely have enough control over enough resource to accomplish our job. We lack budget and people resource. When we look at what management and others expect from us and our alliance, we fall woefully short of resource. We often have significant responsibility with insufficient authority. One of the most important things we *do* have is our ability to persuade others to support our alliance's objectives. On our bad days, even this "persuasion thing" feels like "nothing."

"… in the *eye of a hurricane*" – Here are the chaotic components of the hurricane we get to work in:

- Formal **alliance reviews** – planning, preparation, analysis, calendar coordination, running meetings, follow-up reports, and action item follow-up.

- **Spontaneous high-priority interrupts** – alliance-related update requests for executives, press and industry analysts, reviews of marketing and sales collateral, customer briefings, calls from the partner, escalations within the alliance and escalations from our respective sales organizations.

- A broad range of **internal stakeholders**, all keenly interested in seeing *their* results from our alliance.

- **Traditional business distractions** – standard training courses, unrelenting meetings, performance reviews, administrative overhead, expense reports, travel requests, vacation time and internal "junk" e-mail.

- **Organizational churn** coupled with **personal angst**. Office gossip and water cooler chit-chat. Is there any company that is not reorganizing, downsizing, growing too fast, or being acquired? Who is secure in their job?
- Complexities, difficulties and **challenges in alliancing** (ref: Chapters 2 and 3).

Alliance management is one of the most strategically important jobs in all of business. Effective business relationships are fundamental to the operation of globally-distributed supply chains. These supply chains enable companies to stay focused on their differentiating core competencies while continuing to grow. Alliances can help businesses discover new value-creation opportunities. And the lessons learned in effective strategic alliance management can help transform other business relationships and the world of businesses in general.

Traditional Default Assumptions – problematic role comparisons

In the traditional areas of business, managers can easily make assumptions about the role of alliance manager. If these assumptions drive staffing decisions they will adversely impact the alliance, not with catastrophic outcomes, but with suboptimal results (continued status quo) – good decisions that impede greatness.

The points raised below are not intended to denigrate anyone who works in these areas of business. Nor is it to suggest that these staffing situations always have mediocre results. But if we miss the mark in terms of clearly understanding this role, then effective alliance management will remain elusive.

Account Management – an account manager oversees inter-company business relationships where one company sells to or buys from another. Sales representatives are personally driven toward concrete near-term results. They seek out immediate *exchanges* of product or service for revenue. To equate alliance management with sales is simplistic, short-sighted and dilutes the importance of focusing on *longer*-term and *intangible* forms of value. Sales people often overlook value-creation opportunities.

On the other side of sales is procurement. An alliance manager cannot be too focused on the *acquisition* of value either. Such acquisition can take the form of technology, channel, or a complementary product, all very important to a business. But if there is no *long-term value-creation*, it is not a strategic alliance. The person playing that role is not a strategic alliance manager.

Not all external relationships are equal. Staffing an alliance with someone oriented toward value-*exchange* (either sales or procurement) or value-*extraction* (pure investment relations) can create an unhealthy, lopsided alliance. The competencies required to successfully manage one type of external business relationship do not automatically map to another type of business relationship.

Business Development often focuses primarily on co-marketing and "sell with" programs, admittedly very important aspects of an alliance. But if one accepts that a strategic alliance *creates* significant incremental value, co-marketing alone may be insufficient.

The integration of two companies' products may bring incremental value to customers via a more complete solution. But product integration alone tends to be of marginal long-term value. Therefore, the co-marketing of two loosely-integrated products is a tactical (not strategic) relationship. If the companies provide a *highly-valued* integration, coupled with unique professional services, that tactical relationship starts becoming strategic. This illustrates a demarcation point between tactical relationships and strategic alliances.

Compared to sales and procurement, business development often concerns itself more with value-creation. But alliance managers have a longer-term perspective and our role spans the entire company. Alliance managers differ from business development in degree – we have a longer-term and broader perspective.

Program Management – good program management is critical to the success of large alliances. Given both alliance management and program management span most functional areas and levels in an organization, it can be challenging to clearly differentiate these two roles. One point of differentiation is that an alliance manager is peaked in *relationship* competencies. And it can be helpful to think of an alliance manager as being a mini-CEO – responsible for the overall success of an alliance. In such a model the program manager is then the alliance's mini-COO – responsible for operations and program execution.

This table summarizes the impact of assuming that the nontraditional role of alliance manager is similar to traditional jobs.

Traditional Roles	Similarities to Alliance Managers	Differences Compared to Alliance Managers	Value-Limiting Impact on an Alliance
Account Manager (sales or procurement)	• External relationships	• Value-exchange • Near-term results	• Overlooks long-term value-creation • Becomes a tactical relationship
Business Development	• Oriented toward value	• Weak in relationships • Near-term results • Tangible value	• Weak in long-term value-creation • Becomes a tactical relationship
Program Manager	• Can span most of the business	• Scope limited to a program – time-bound, organizationally-bound • Limited experience in relationships	• Loss of long-term perspective • Missed value-creation opportunities • Weak collaborative relationship • Becomes a tactical relationship

Table 5.3 – Comparing traditional default role assumptions with the role of alliance manager, impacts on alliance.

The result of attempting to use any of these three traditional business roles to fulfill the nontraditional role of alliance manager may be the diminishment of an alliance's strategic impact. That business relationship will become more tactical than strategic – the time dimension gets shortened and less value gets created. These relationships will remain important to the business. But they will miss their potential for greatness.

Unhealthy Value-Stifling Behaviors – problem

There are behaviors which are unhealthy in any alliance. They stifle our ability to find and create new value. These behaviors are often more self-serving than other-serving. They do not serve the alliance.

When we are confused about our role, we can end up acting out in unhealthy ways. We then damage ourselves and our alliance. At these times we can benefit from the honest loving help of a "trusted other." We need someone to point out our unhealthy behaviors so we can change and grow.

Look at the following humorously entitled behaviors – but with serious internal reflection. Do you recognize any of this, in yourself or others? We can have fun while we go deep.

Drama Queen – some days we are overwhelmed by challenge. Peers in the organization do not understand what we do. We are, after all, trying to "do the impossible with nothing in the eye of a hurricane." Given the cultural and strategic chasms that exist between the companies, the behavior of the other side adds unique challenges. When we cannot understand another's behavior, we easily assume it to be grounded in deviousness, incompetency or craziness. In the midst of frustration and self-doubt, we may be tempted to highlight the other side's odd behaviors and reinforce how tough our job is in order to get sympathy. Ultimately, we are seeking respect in an unhealthy manner.

Sometimes we catch ourselves saying, "Wait until you hear what *they* did today. You won't believe it!" On these days when too much challenge comes our way, we may say, "Enough!" If someone asks us to do something new, we might melodramatically say, "I am too busy," meaning, "I am stressed out and overloaded. So, back off!"

In a sick way we may actually enjoy the drama of our job. This drama can gives us an artificial sense of purpose. Drama makes our job seem more difficult and, thus, more important. In some ways drama can be a form of addiction. Being with an addict or being around drama all the time can be tiring. It distracts us from our core work, and it can repel others from wanting to work in our alliance.[43]

Complexity King – a close relative of the Drama Queen. Instead of using drama to make our job look difficult and important, we use complexity. Our job is complex enough. We do not need to give complexity excess emphasis. If we want ourselves and our alliance to be more successful, we actually need to make things simpler. Not simplistic, but simpler – more focused. As Einstein said, we should make things as simple as possible but not simpler.

We may notice ourselves unconsciously slipping into the addiction of complexity when we say to others, "You just would not understand, this situation is *too* complex." If we cannot describe something in a simple manner, easily understandable by others, then we ourselves are lost. We are lost in the forest of complexity; we can see the trees but not the forest's big picture view.

Addiction to complexity has the same type of adverse effects on self and the alliance as addiction to drama. It distracts us from our core issues. It can easily orient us toward being more self-serving than other-serving. We then end up embodying and propagating a counter-productive spirit.

Fear-Monger – is a cousin of the Drama Queen, using a more poignant form of drama. When we are in fear-monger mode we focus on a specific partner or partnering in general. We fear our company will be taken advantage of. This may occur between a smaller and bigger partner, where the smaller one feels they may get put out of business or be acquired. There are certain companies, like Microsoft, Google or Wal-Mart, where even the mention of their name stirs up fear and a sense of awe for those who manage those relationships.

Clearly we need to be protective of our intellectual property, revenues and assets. We need to make sure we are not being taken advantage of. But when taken to the extreme such fears become self-serving to the alliance manager. We have to ask ourselves, "*Why* am I emphasizing this particular issue? What are my motives? Is this issue being discussed to be resolved or so I can be revered?" Generating or exacerbating fear, like creating drama and complexity, distracts us from the core issues where attention should be focused. Fear sours the climate in an alliance, making collaboration harder.

Information Hoarder – "Information is power, so hold onto it!" That phrase is accepted in business as "truth," something we need to accept as reality. Well, it is the *wrong* sort of reality for alliance managers.

Value is derived from shared ideas. Ideas are currency in an alliance's economic system. This economy grows when ideas are shared, extended and used. Just like the flow of currency helps an economy grow, the flow of ideas helps an alliance grow. We absolutely do need to protect our company's intellectual property, of course. But paradoxically, alliance managers need to *freely give* away our most precious alliance-improving ideas.

It is not unreasonable for us to actually strive to obsolete ourselves in this area. This idea runs counter to traditional business thought. But we discover, through our personal experiences, that the best thing for our alliance is to *give away* our best ideas to as many people as will hear them and use them. These ideas include:

- How to bridge cultural differences and engage more effectively with the other company.

- How to bridge the strategic chasm between the companies to better understand possibilities.

- Understanding each company's organization, products, technologies, customers and competitors.

- Understanding each company's decision-making and resource-committing processes.

- How to deepen relationship and bring more trust in the alliance.

The more these ideas are freely and broadly shared, the better. If this information is hoarded, the alliance suffers, it stays stuck in status quo mediocrity, and we fail.

This sounds unbelievable but we actually *choose* these unhealthy behaviors. We may not be consciously aware of these choices. But if we look deeply at our inner-most motives, we can see why these behaviors are unhealthy. If our behaviors are about promoting ourselves, we obscure value and adversely affect the overall climate in an alliance. So we ask ourselves, "Are we trying to advance *ourselves* or the *alliance*?" There may be other unhealthy behaviors. We can recognize them all by striving to understand their underlying motives.

Unhealthy Behaviors	Impact on the Alliance	Impact on Us Personally
Drama Queen	• Focused on problems, distractive • Creates a tiresome, draining climate	• Gives a temporary boost in importance • Distracts us from our core issues
Complexity King	• Focused on complexity, distractive • Vision of opportunity is obscured	• Self-serving, rather than other-serving • Embodies the wrong spirit; we are lost
Fear-Monger	• Undermines collaboration • Sours the overall climate	• A temporary boost in importance • Distracts us from our core issues
Information Hoarder	• Directly stifles value-creation • Encourages a "me vs. you" climate	• A false gain in personal power • Misuse of informational power; we fail

Table 5.4 – Unhealthy behaviors that stifle value-creation.

Value-Limiting Traps – problem

Even if we are aligned with management on job description, we can still miss the mark. We can fall into other unproductive behaviors beyond those discussed in the prior section. There may be times when the behaviors covered in this section are necessary, but if they are used long-term they constrain value-creation. They should be used sparingly, only when absolutely needed. Inexperienced alliance managers may be enticed to use these behaviors longer than necessary.

Gatekeeper – as a new alliance manager we might think, "I need to be in *every* meeting and involved in *all* communication." We may even feel a bit defensive when something good happens without our direct involvement. In such situations our initial reaction might come from fear – maybe we are not *needed*. At these times we can feel threatened *because* we were not aware of all the activities happening in our alliance. What is our role and value to the organization if good things can happen *without* us?

If we try to sustain a gatekeeper role, we will burn out. We alienate others by implicitly distrusting them. Why else would we feel like we need to be everywhere? If we "succeed" at being a gatekeeper, the restriction on information flow will impede value-creation in the alliance. As the alliance manager we *do* need to be "all-knowing." It is appropriate for us to be in the know; ultimately, this is how we stay in control. But our best knowing and controlling comes via nontraditional and indirect means.

Dictator – the dictator role is a logical extension of the controlling gatekeeper role. There may be extreme situations when we find dictatorship to be warranted. During a major customer escalation or when immediate action is needed, dictating is necessary and helpful. But done to excess or at inappropriate times, this behavior comes at a high cost to interpersonal relations and the alliance. It drives people away, rather than attracts. It can be demoralizing for our "lowly servants." It damages the overall environment in our alliance. Ultimately, dictators are over-thrown during an insurgency.

If we remain dictators, our days will be numbered. We can guarantee personal and organizational frustration, and ultimately job loss.

Executive Liaison – executive-level relations are critical in any alliance. We must effectively and confidently work with executives in both companies. Executive meetings need to be focused with appropriate preparation. There needs to be strong action item follow-up, often directly with these executives.

The risk here is to simplistically assume that if the executives agree, then the results will happen. All we have to do is get executive-level handshakes, issue a joint press release, and our job is done. This ignores the importance of our on-going working at *all* levels and in all functional areas of our alliance. There does need to be clear high-level alignment and focus on the shared business objectives. This alignment needs to pervade *throughout* the alliance, not only among executives. We should also share with executives the alliance's vision and the alliance's successes and use executives as escalation-point-of-last-resort when all else fails. Executives cannot be our predominate area of focus. If we rely on our executives too much, we will avoid the people who actually *do* the work and we will fail.

Escalation Manager – we *do* need to proactively resolve problematic situations. We need to think clearly under fire and lead others toward positive resolution. More important than *resolving* escalations is *prevention*. In the world of business we might hear the cynical statement, "It is better to put out a fire than to prevent one – you get better performance reviews as a highly-visible firefighter. Fire preventers are not seen, and so they're not rewarded for their proactive work." This short-sighted, self-serving mindset is problematic in a strategic alliance.

Escalation management cannot be our primary job. There is also the risk of placing so much attention on problem-prevention that more important areas get ignored. This becomes counterproductive. With excess attention placed on problems they *will* be found, to the distraction of finding value.

Schmoozing Drone – the Germans have a name for this

role, "Frühstücksdirektor" or "Director of breakfast." It is true that without interpersonal relationships there is no alliance. But socializing and entertainment cannot be our primary focus. We cannot just work on meetings, dinners, get-togethers, team-building and social events. We need to be about value.

A drone bee's primary purpose in life is to wait. Drones wait for the hive to swarm and for the hatching of a new queen bee. Then all the drones race for the single opportunity to mate with the queen and then they die. A drone has a once-in-a-lifetime opportunity to make a difference. As alliance managers we should be *continually* making a difference, with *value* as our objective. Value is both our means *and* our end. The best way to build strong interpersonal relations is to *be* of value – to personally deliver value, to everyone, everywhere, always. So we need to be worker bees, not drones.

Socializing, or creating a sense of community, is best achieved by working collectively on value.

Organizational Concierge – being everyone's gofer, "Do this. Find out about that."

Thinking of us as being the concierge to our alliance is the right service-oriented mindset. The question is, "What does *great* service look like from the alliance manager to their alliance?"

The risk is that we can too easily use the concierge idea to the detriment of ourselves and our alliance. If *all* we are doing is servicing concierge requests, we are inadvertently being distracted from the strategically-critical need to lead. The alliance and the business need us to lead the alliance. Alliance leadership is like no other leadership in business – it is counterintuitive and non-traditional in its approach, attitude & mindset, skills and knowledge. We need to be very careful that we don't use concierge service requests as a seductive distraction from our challenging and important leadership work.

If we find ourselves saying, "I have too many urgent demands from others in the alliance; I don't have time to do planning and leadership work," then our days are out-of-balance and our alliance is suffering as a result. We are suffering from doing good things at the expense of doing great things. We need to decide what we need

Role Clarity – who am I?

to say "no" to so we can say "yes" to our transformational work.

Alliance management is definitely about service. It is about the right kind of service that will take the alliance to higher levels of effectiveness. It is about service that will lead the alliance toward greater value creation. Perhaps this title simply needs to be relabeled "value-focused concierge." The question is then, "How can we provide service that will enable the alliance to be most value-creative?"

Value-Limiting Traps	Impact on the Alliance	Impact on us Personally
Gatekeeper	• Restricts information flow • Reduces value-creation	• "Burn out" • Strained interpersonal relations
Dictator	• Demoralizes people in alliance • Drives others away	• Frustration as others don't obey us • Likely loss of job
Executive Liaison	• Poor results as lower-levels of the organization are ignored	• Frustration as things don't "just happen" • Possible loss of job
Escalation Manager	• Problem- not value-oriented alliance • Value is obscured by problems	• Negative outlook as we obsessively look for problems, which we *do* find • Becomes *the* problem
Schmoozing Drone	• Little impact – a NOP[44] • Maybe a once-in-a-lifetime opportunity	• Waits and watches others create • Stagnation and frustration
Organizational Concierge	• Good (not great) service-orientation • Weakened alliance leadership	• Not serving in most value-enabling way – seen as the alliance's "gofer"

Table 5.5 – Value-limiting traps – behaviors possibly needed at times, but with value-limiting impact on the alliance.

The behaviors in Figure 5.5 trap us into situations that limit value. If we pay attention we will notice other problematic or unhealthy behaviors. We must recognize them for what they are; otherwise, we will be distracted from our true role and our alliance will get stuck at mediocre levels of value-creation. We can recognize value-limiting behaviors by boldly looking within ourselves and examining our real motives. For example, are we motivated by "what's in it for *me*?" or "what's in it for *we*?" Are we motivated to serve or get? Are we trying to look good or do what's right for the alliance?

We can also recognize the unhealthiness of our behaviors by the affect they have, or will have, on our alliance. As alliance managers our unhealthy behaviors end up limiting value-creation in our alliance, either near-term or longer-term.

The tone of this chapter now shifts from problem toward solution.

The Negotiator Role – a pervasive solution

If we think of negotiating as a role we only play at certain times we miss a huge opportunity. Think of negotiating as synonymous with "important discussion." We do want our discussions to be important and impactful. To limit negotiating to certain times and events limits its value to us and our alliance.

Negotiating is not an exercise in hostility. It does not require us to aggressively extract concessions out of another. It is not about finding compromise between positions. The most effective negotiators have developed a unique set of nontraditional skills and a collaborative attitude & mindset.[45] They create a trust-filled environment around them that enables open and in-depth exploratory discussions. They focus on what is core and critical, ignoring the rest. They have the capacity to straddle between apparently opposing ideas or thoughts:

- They can simultaneously be **empathetic and assertive** – soft on people, hard on issues.

- They can persuasively **argue for either side** – they can represent either side's fundamental objectives and key underlying interests with equal logic and passion – they can see either, or, and both.

- They are **structured** and methodical while also being **open and receptive** – they are comfortable in a state of bounded instability or controlled chaos.
- They can tap into the **creativity** that **lies between** two apparently irreconcilable ideas – when others are willing to settle for a compromise between positions, the average of "a" and "b," the most effective negotiators realize there is a yet-to-be-discovered "c" that is different and better than compromise – they can seek and find a creative third option which can only be found "in the between" between "a" and "b" – open healthy confrontational debate is great, the more we stay squarely in the midst, in the *between,* between positions and ideas.
- They seek the enthusiasm and inspiration that also resides **in the** *between***.*

Negotiating skills training is clearly helpful. Negotiating will naturally become more effective as we also develop alliance-oriented and relationship-fostering skills. This competency is helpful every day and throughout our alliance. Negotiating is about having deep, substantive and impactful discussions. This is something we want more of in our alliance.

As we have the trust to openly explore creative options based on a deep understanding of both sides, we will find and create more and more value.

Negotiating is not just a role. At its best, the most effective negotiating is *a state of being.*

A "Mini-CEO" – a concretely limiting solution

Comparing our role with that of a CEO is an interesting thought exercise. As summarized in the table below, there are important similarities between CEO and alliance manager. Both have to work effectively across the entire business. Both have to work throughout the lifecycle of product and service development – from R&D-to-Marketing-to-Sales. They both have to work with legal, finance and human resource departments. Both CEOs and alliance managers run a business. A good alliance manager views their alliance as their business. We should bear responsibility for the business results of our alliance.

However, the differences between these two roles are stark. A CEO typically has enough resource and budget at their disposal. The alliance manager is often resource-starved. CEOs tend to focus more on the near-term and tangible forms of value. Alliance managers often have a more expanded view of value – considering longer-term and less tangible forms. CEOs make decisions. Alliance managers influence decisions. The CEO has tremendous formal power. Alliance managers have limited formal power. We can have significant informal power obtained through the art of subtle persuasion and the practice of self-obsolescence.[46]

Some might say it is grandiose, dangerous and reckless to compare ourselves to a CEO; others may say that it is too frustrating to compare our job with that of a CEO. But if we think deeply about comparing these roles and reflect upon what we *can* accomplish via *nontraditional means*, we see that thinking of ourselves as *just* a CEO in many ways actually short-changes our true potential. Rather than focusing on what a CEO has that we *do not have*, we should deeply consider what we *do have* at our disposal.

We need to focus on seeing what we *can* accomplish with what we *do* have to work with. We will then be astounded to see the resources that *are* available to us to increase our *informal* power and *indirect* influence. It is actually nice to have such a focus imposed on us by necessity; such is the compelling effect love has on us. Love compels us to grow; and our focused attention is powerful.

Comparing the CEO and Alliance Manager Roles	
Similarities	Differences
<ul><li>Both span entire lifecycle – from R&D-to-Sales – plus legal and finance</li><li>Both are oriented toward creating incremental value for the business</li></ul>	<ul><li>CEO has control over significant budget and resource</li><li>CEO tends to be more focused on near-term tangible value</li><li>CEO has direct decision-making authority</li><li>CEO has more formal power and direct authority</li></ul><ul><li>Alliance Manager has insufficient budget and resource</li><li>Alliance Manager considers near- and long-term, tangible and intangible forms of value</li><li>Alliance Manager mostly influences decisions</li><li>Alliance Manager has informal power – subtle persuasion</li></ul>
Conclusions	
<ul><li>You may feel limited in comparing yourself to a CEO in terms of power, authority and resource.</li><li>By comparing yourself to a CEO you may end up *limiting* your own *thinking* and:</li><li>Miss the opportunity to tenaciously focus on *only* the *core* and *nontraditional* to do our job.</li><li>Obscure the necessitated-opportunity to focus on *attitude & mindset* to deepen *relationship*.</li><li>Miss the *expansion* of our *informal power* via the vast nontraditional means at our disposal; such informal power can often exceed formal power – e.g., when the CEO asks for 'permission.'</li></ul>	

Table 5.7 – Comparing ourselves to a CEO is self-limiting thinking.

Do not focus on what you do *not* have; focus on what you *do* have – accept it, embrace it and then use it. This concept may seem too abstract to be of practical value to you. If so, maybe spend more time with Table 5.7.

Consider someone with a disability, someone who is blind. If they focus on what they do not have, they will miss their opportunity to develop what they *do* have. If they focus on their loss of sight, they will not develop great hearing skills. By focusing their attention on what they do have, they develop those skills to a level others can only imagine. Those *nontraditional* skills become strengths that compensate for what they lack.

Look squarely at what we as alliance managers *have* at our disposal. What we really have are (a) ourselves, (b) others and (c) relationships. With this focus we are forced to develop *nontraditional* skills – the ability to change attitude & mindset in order to deepen relationships. With this restricted focus, we accomplish amazing things others can only dream of. This is how we enable greater value-creation.

So, thinking of our role as a "mini-CEO" is actually limiting. We end up limiting ourselves.

If you think you are a "mini-CEO" … *think again!*

Agents of Change – adaptive solution

The core ideas in this section are derived from *Change the World: How Ordinary People Can Accomplish Extraordinary Results* by Robert E Quinn.[47] His ideas have been adapted to the role of alliance manager.

You might ask, "Why are we thinking about comparing our role to that of an agent of change?" If, as alliance managers, we are *not* about changing our alliance, our company and ourselves, we might ask, "Why are we doing this job?" Change is absolutely needed if we are to turn around the current rate of failure in alliances and transform our frustrations into enthusiasm and joy. Creating value itself is an act of change.

Quinn's book describes four models of change agents, summarized in Appendix A of his book. We will apply these change agent types to the role of strategic alliance manager. From my experience I can now see how I have evolved through these four types in progressive stages in my career.[48] This is not to say that transformational change agents are the best and more advanced than fact-based or "telling" change agents. In fact, it seems like there are daily opportunities to apply each of these four types, depending on a given situation. The important thing is for us to be comfortable playing any of these roles, as situations dictate.

Read Table 5.8 in a clockwise manner. Agents of change tend to progress from *fact-based* to *authority-based* to *relationship-based* and, finally, to *transformational*. The outer ring illustrates how a certain type of change agent is most effective during a major activity or phase of alliance development.

	Assessment	Structured Control	Escalation	
Due Diligence	**Fact-based** Behaviors we embody: • Arguments of **rational persuasion** • Be an expert with all the necessary facts and knowledge • Lead sufficiently detailed analysis in preparation for discussion and negotiation • Instruct, inform and teach	**Authority-based** Behaviors we embody: • **Leverage behavior** to force compliance • Use authority, and if necessary fear, to legitimize directives • Assure compliance via performance-based reward and punishment • Information flow and context is controlled		Preservation
	Transformational Our embodiment: • **Transform self** – embrace hypocrisy, spiritual boldness, lead by being • Productive community, transcends external sanctions, disrupts systems (as needed) • Collective awareness of and surrender to emergent reality – "something going on"	**Relationship-based** Behaviors we embody: • **Open** all-inclusive and clear **dialogue** fostered in a supportive environment • Healthy non-judgmental confrontation to resolve important and difficult issues • Interpersonal cohesion – feeling "part of" • Strong emphasis on win/win relationship		
	Trail Blaze	Transform & Renew	Negotiation	

Table 5.8 – Alliance managers as agents of change.

Fact-based – "If I give you enough information, you will change."

In this role we focus on educating, informing and even dictating in order to *make* change happen. The belief is that if we just present all the facts, others will be persuaded to cooperate and change. In this mode the focus is on developing basic competencies and becoming a knowledgeable expert. Detailed analysis is important so that any questioning or criticism can be effectively counter-argued, given it is grounded in fact.

This mode of operation helps in the assessment of work. Often collective attention needs to be focused on critical technical, legal or regulatory matters. When used in combination with the transformational mode, being fact-based is helpful during due diligence assessments of new partnering opportunities. When combined with the authoritative mode, fact-based is helpful when highly-structured control is necessary, like an alliance in the pharmaceutical industry.

Authority-based – "If I am your manager, or if I 'escalate' to your manager, I can *make* you change."

We often strive for greater personal authority by moving to a higher level in the organization. The belief is that our personal frustration can be mitigated with more authority, a larger team or increased budget. What we think we need is more leverage. Title and position are important. It is crucial to have concise directives, backed up with the unambiguous ability to award and punish others in order to achieve organizational alignment and individual compliance. Control of information is important to maintain; leverage needs to be maintained so information-hoarding seems necessary.

This mode helps in the middle of a major customer escalation, when both strict control and immediate action is needed. Coupled with being fact-based, positional authority helps structure alliance activity. Combined with the relationship-based mode, this mode helps during times when the alliance is threatened, like when one of the partners is being acquired by another company. A regulatory audit may also seem threatening to an alliance. During these times discussions need to be open and trustful, but also controlled.

Relationship-based – "As we work together, we will both change."

Over time, we begin to realize "it is all about relationship." Participatory dialogue becomes important. There is a strong focus on the human processes: open dialogue, supportive communication, and the need to assure that everyone's position is heard. There is commitment to a win/win alliance, where both sides benefit. Equality in "gives and gets" is important – we strive for a balance-of-trade. With a desire to maintain a positive relationship, conflict and confrontation may be suppressed. As we gain experience we realize that *loving confrontation* – jointly facing issues *in* the relationship without conflict, without attacking each other – is healthy and necessary.

With an extreme obsession on relationship there may come an unhealthy tendency toward striving to *always* achieve 100% consensus in *all* decisions. This is a simplistic form of listening to the voice of the collective that can stifle forward movement with suboptimal decisions. The collective's voice needs to be heard, but it also needs to be tempered with a clear and passionate vision of the future. Leaders use their vision to filter, refine and focus what is heard from the collective. As I see it, this is related to how healthy leadership occurs in the rooms of AA or NA (in 12-step recovery) where a single point of decision making and accountability is responsible for allowing group conscience to be heard. After that they make decisions and take steps on behalf of the group. Their vision is grounded in being of service to newcomers, helping them find freedom from addiction and a new way to live.

A strong bias toward relationship is helpful during the early phase of formal negotiations or during the establishment of a new alliance. Combined with the authority-based mode, a relationship focus is helpful when an alliance feels threatened. Combined with the transformation mode, a relationship focus is helpful in the transformation or renewal of an alliance.

Transformational – "In order for me to change you, *I must first change me;* and, you might never change."

At the height of our personal and organizational effectiveness, we see ourselves as an integral part of the collective whole. We realize that we play a very *small* role, and also, paradoxically, a very *large* role. As individuals it is all about us and nothing about us – it is all about "we." Others produce the tangible value. We, as alliance managers, simply and powerfully enable that value to be effectively created; to do this we focus on the *invisible* and the *timeless*.

We realize that we need to personally embody growth and progress. We grow to personify the common good of our alliance community. We are empowered as we empower others – as we give, we receive. We are empowered by our team to lead the way over obstacles and through value-impediments. The alliance team's possible disruption of the greater business organization may be inevitable, again for the greater good. As alliance managers, we have the opportunity to "*be* the metaphor for metamorphosis."

The transformational mode is most helpful as we are "trail blazing" or looking for breakthroughs in the alliance. Coupled with the relationship-based mode, it helps when we need to transform or reinvent the alliance. Combined with fact-based mode, it helps when we are conducting due diligence assessment of a new opportunity.

Clearly the transformational mode of alliance management may not be helpful all of the time and in every situation. It can actually be quite tiring to stay transformational, tiring for us and for those around us. It is important that we are comfortable being in any mode, including transformational, as situations dictate, as opportunities present themselves.

The **three traditional types** of change agents (*fact*-, *authority*- and *relationship*-based) primarily focus on the acquisition and use of *knowledge* or *skill* development, not so much on attitude & mindset.

Changing *attitude & mindset* accomplishes **transformation**. To become transformational we have to be willing to change our perception of self, others and life. We accomplish this by *first going within*, and then by going out into our alliance community. Transformation, like life, is "a we thing" – we cannot do it alone.

Alliance Managers as Transformational Change Agents

Fundamental premise: greater good comes through collaboration. Therefore, great alliances focus on making collaboration great. As alliance managers we struggle to create a more value-producing climate, while surrounded by a world obsessed with competition and pervaded by fear. In alliancing, a competitive mindset immediately puts the alliance's environment into a "me vs. you" mode or a scarcity mindset, while collaboration focuses on expanding business in abundance.

> *In any human-based system, more is accomplished through* collaboration *focused on* abundance *than through* competition *and* fear *focused on dividing a fixed resource.*

At a minimum there needs to be a balance between being competitive and being collaborative. Today's business world is out-of-balance with an obsession on competition, to the point of organizational and individual dysfunction. Perhaps the world of business has reached a phase in its growth where its nearly singular focus on competition and winning at all costs has run its course. To take companies to the next level of value-creating performance, collaboration needs to be fostered.

Spiritual Principles in Strategic Alliances

We as alliance managers are at the forefront of a fundamental shift in the world of business.

Our personal vision sees ourselves as leaders helping transform business from today's fear-based, me vs. you, scarcity climate into a healthier environment of rejuvenation, abundance and greater growth. Alliance managers have a unique role to affect this change. We are individuals striving to accelerate the creation of incremental business value via collaboration.

This is the ultimate disruption of the system, as we help change the world of business for its own good and to its own greatness.

Our Relationship with (the Attributes of) Deity – a thoughtful solution, leading to grandeur

Hopefully what is suggested below is not seen as blasphemous. These concepts are suggested in order to open us up to the grand possibilities in ourselves and in our jobs as alliance managers.

So far we have talked about (a) value-creation, (b) doing the impossible and (c) changing the climate in our alliance. Creating, accomplishing the impossible, and changing climate are things that deity or gods do. Perhaps we might benefit from a reflection on *our relationship* with the *idea of deity*, the creative force of the Universe. Traditional definitions say that this divine force has three basic characteristics; the divine is:

- Omnipotent – *being all-powerful*
- Omnipresent – *being ever-present*
- Omniscient – *being all-knowing*

If alliances are to be value-creating and we have to do the impossible and change the very climate in our alliance, it might be helpful to consider *our relationship* with these *divine ideas*.

Omnipotent – *our power & resources*

In business, power takes on two forms: (a) the ability to commit organizational resources – *formal* power, and (b) the influence of others – *informal* power.

As alliance managers our *formal* power is finite. We typically have insufficient formal power in our own company, and no formal power in the other company.

Our informal power, or the ability to influence others, is derived from the impact our *ideas* have on others. Our attitude & mindset determines *what* we do with our ideas. Do we *give* or *hoard* our ideas? The resultant power derived from giving our ideas away actually determines what we *accomplish* with our ideas.

This informal idea-based form of power actually *grows* when *shared*. Our *informal* power is *limitless*.

Omnipresent – *our presence & influence*

New alliance managers try to be personally present everywhere – in all meetings, in all communications, and in all conference calls. While this behavior is understandable, it stifles the flow of information. The alliance manager becomes an information bottleneck.

Alliance managers can, and should, achieve ever-present influence in an entirely different form.

As we grow in our ability to be of service to individuals throughout the alliance, as we share our knowledge, wisdom and insights with others, our personal influence will pervade the alliance. People will grow to understand and support our vision. Our perspective on issues and opportunities will be seen, understood and accepted by others. When we cannot be physically present in meetings or directly involved in communications, people will ask, "What would she think about this situation? How would she respond?" Or they might say, "Let's check in with her before we make our final decision." They will naturally extend your vision throughout the alliance – whether or not you are physically present. This epitomizes success in the art of *virtual presence* and *indirect influence.*

Omniscient – *our all-knowing wisdom*

Alliance managers are expected to be 'all-knowing' about the state of the alliance. At any time and with anyone, we need to be able to succinctly answer such questions as:

- What is the value of this alliance? What are our major opportunities? What is the vision?
- What are the impediments standing in the way of the value? What are our major challenges and obstacles? How can I help?
- What is working? What is not working? What should we do differently?

Upper-management may ask at any time, "How is the alliance?" We should always be able to provide them with the best answer. They expect us to enable everyone who works in the alliance. We enable others to be as effective as possible by providing them with practical recommendations for spanning the cultural and strategic chasms. Management expects us to be as all-sharing with this knowledge and wisdom as is judicious and reasonable: obviously, confidential information must be handled with care, and too much information overwhelms others.

As alliance managers we have the unique opportunity to experience personal growth in power and presence, derived from idea-sharing. It has been said that the best teachers strive to obsolete themselves – they want their students to surpass them. This sentiment helps in alliancing, too.

We want those who work in our alliance not to need us; they will then *want* us more.

I have experimented with "self-obsolescence" by sharing *all* I could with *whomever* I could, *whenever* I could. The result was an *increase* in personal power and influence on both sides of the alliance. This personal development tact is counterintuitive. It may appear to many in the world of business as career suicide. It flies in the face of traditional logic that says "information is power – so hoard it."[49]

Hoarded ideas lose their power to influence and help. In contrast, as ideas are shared, they grow. When we *give away* our ideas we do not lose them. In fact, they grow in the process of sharing. There is a natural tendency by the receiver to share back. Individuals and organizations benefit, and our influence as alliance manager expands. Shared ideas enable value-creation in the alliance. In a virtuous cycle, as we give we grow in personal value, power and influence; all of this is based on shared knowledge and appreciation.

This type of informal power can actually end up being *greater* than formal power. Others may come to us for guidance and direction, and even permission. We need to use this power in humility; but, paradoxically, with great boldness, too. We must be focused on doing the greatest good for all concerned – to help all grow.

With this particular source of informal power comes lonesome responsibility. Often we may be the only ones who see certain situations and opportunities. We may be the only ones with a relatively objective perspective. This insight may require us to take unpopular stances. We may have to help others see what we see, so that the organization can make the most informed decisions.

Achieving the all-knowing *attribute of deity should be our primary purpose.*

As ideas are extended to others our informal power increases. This type of power broadens our presence and deepens our influence throughout our alliance.

Negotiating with Your Greatest Spiritual Teacher – Negotiating with the Infinite

What would it be like if tomorrow you had a negotiating meeting with your greatest spiritual teacher? What if you had a face-to-face meeting with Buddha, Christ, Gandhi, Abraham, Luther or the Dalai Lama? Or what if you were going to negotiate with deity? This last scenario might be called our "day of reckoning." What would that be like? Deep reflection on this idea brings a sense of focused and intense presence.

Imagining your negotiation with deity raises some interesting questions:

- How would you **prepare**? On what topics or issues would you focus your attention during preparation?

- Would you be **fully present** during the meeting? Would you be checking e-mail or talking on your mobile phone? What would be the nature of your presence? Where would you be focusing your attention? Would they be paying attention to you? Would you be giving them your full attention?

- What would the **discussion** to be like? Would the discussions be not only intense and focused but also **loving**? Would **core issues** get addressed? If so, how would they be addressed?

- When deity eloquently **argues both sides** of an issue, can you imagine asking yourself "Whose side is deity on?" So, whose side is deity on? Subsequently, if we want to be excellent negotiators in our role as alliance manager, whose side should *we* be on?

- Would the **results** of this meeting be balanced? Would creative solutions surface during the meeting, ideas that no one had previously considered? Would the results "stand the test of time?"

- Would we be **enthused** and **inspired** after the meeting? Would we be uplifted and motivated to passionately accomplish the agreed upon action items?

- Would it be a good meeting or a **great meeting**? Why? What made the difference?

- Perhaps there is a place for divine principles in our job. A great spiritual teacher whom many revere as personifying the Divine said, "Ye are gods."[50]

Suggested Job Description – be a focused solution

Obviously, your actual job description is finalized with your manager. The following ideas may stir up new thoughts and deepen those discussions.

Referring back to the key points from Chapter 4, we develop these priorities for our job:

1. Improve **attitude & mindset** in order to deepen **relationship**.
    a. **know Self, be true to Self** – self-confidence, self-assurance, self-acceptance – first go within, embrace hypocrisy, heal personal integrity gaps
    b. embody **enthusiasm**, inspiration and enlightenment – seek out what is *within*: Self, others and relationship
    c. learn, embody and **use simple truths**[51]
        i. simplicity in the midst of complexity – simplicity on the other side of complexity
        ii. view others as Self; part of a productive community (one)
        iii. stay in the moment; presence; focus (now)
        iv. creativity (our divine nature)
        v. creative mindfulness (our thoughts create)
        vi. optimism; choose to overlook the bad and see only the good (love)
2. **Relationship-ize others**: personally embody, demonstrate and teach relationship-deepening behaviors, skills and perspectives to others who are working in the alliance.
    a. conduct **just-enough and just-in-time training**, often subtly and unbeknownst to others
    b. focus self and others on **nontraditional skills**, behaviors, perspectives and knowledge
        i. holistic listening, presence and empathetic rapport-building

Spiritual Principles in Strategic Alliances

- ii. healthy or loving confrontation to call for and, hence, create trust
- iii. focusing collective attention on the simple essence *in* the alliance – incremental value and value-impediments
- iv. self-obsolescence – give to get – provide service to the community – gain informal power and presence via proactively sharing or giving away your best ideas
- v. problems and answers lie within, in the midst – in the alliance, between people, between ideas, between self and spirit – stay in the between – "we"
- vi. collaborative, counterintuitive negotiating – i.e., *The Program on Negotiation* (**www.pon.harvard.edu**) focused on: open high-trust communication, abundance vs. scarcity mindset, creative brainstorming on value-creating options, etc.

c. help others practically **span the cultural and strategic chasms** between the companies

3. **Alliance-ize others' work product**: assure that critical documents embody the subtle nuances of alliancing work.

   a. strategic business plans
      - i. assure that linkages between the corporation's and the alliance's plans are clear – alliance's contribution and support of corporate strategy is clear; alliance's impact on corporate strategy is clear – the alliance is driven by strategy, and not vice versa
      - ii. planners sufficiently understand alliancing – long-term nature, forms of tangible and intangible value, importance of relationship and other unique nontraditional subtleties of alliancing
      - iii. corporate and alliance plans acknowledge *relationship* as a corporate asset – plan for, invest in and measure relationship improvements

iv. there is a clear, committed and funded strategic business plan for the alliance – focused on achieving incremental value vision and overcoming value-impediments; focused on the long-term intangible forms of value, knowing this will lead to near-term tangible forms
   b. financial analysis
      i. acknowledge and quantify all forms of value with special attention on the long-term and intangible forms – done in a manner accepted by finance and management
      ii. develop accepted financial metrics for assessing the corporate asset of relationship
   c. **legal contracts** and **informal teaming agreements**
      i. use both formal (contracts) and informal teaming agreements – balance rigidity vs. flexibility
      ii. acknowledge and manage the unique ambiguities and risks of alliancing
4. **Other: time permitting** and **as needed**, we delve into important areas such as strategic business planning, financial analysis, legal and contractual issues, regulatory issues, competitive analysis, ecosystem analysis, etc. Ideally, this work should be primarily done by others with our input, guidance and perspective.

Given the unique nontraditional role of alliance management, *how* our work is to be done is at least as important as *what* we do. On the next page are thoughts on how we might view, describe or *think about our job*, which affects how we do it.

Spiritual Principles in Strategic Alliances

Strategic Alliance Manager	
Is	**Is not**
• about value-**creation** in all forms • both **long-term** and near-term oriented • a **negotiator** – **always** leading open, high-trust value-discovering discussions • **like a mini-CEO** – but using nontraditional competencies to develop all forms of value • an **agent of change** & **growth** – leading change, first in self – comfortable using a range of change agent roles • a **creator** – a loving, divinely inspired and inspiring, value-creating being • the **embodiment of value** – being of value, always, with everyone, everywhere, give, serve	• **just** about the **exchange** or **extraction** of **tangible** value (esp. just revenue) • focused **just** on **near-term** results • **primarily** an account manager, business development manager or program manager • **addicted** to being a drama queen, complexity king, fear-monger or information hoarder – there is *never* a rational reason for behaving like this; there *is* a better way to live • **always** a gatekeeper, dictator, executive liaison, escalation manager or schmoozing drone – *sometimes* we may need to play some of these roles, but *only* when absolutely needed

Table 5.11 – Strategic Alliance Manager – is and is not.

From the Table 5.11, we can start describing our job.

- To self, and maybe to a few trusted others, we might say:

"In true humility **I am the 'god' of this alliance.** I am about enabling value-creation. I *enable creation* to occur."

This *is* a bold statement, but it is also very empowering and clarifying. It is interesting to reflect on what this idea really means – its impact on self and others. Is it helpful? Does it clarify the role of being an alliance manager?

This statement is not intended to be a statement of self-centered grandiosity, but a statement of *selfless* and *Self-full grandeur*. Our job is *both* "all about me" *and* "nothing about me."

"I am a value-creator. I focus on uncovering, discovering and enabling the *creation* of value. My focus is also on the removal of value-impediments. My job is

Role Clarity – who am I?

best accomplished as I enable and empower others – it is about *me* and it is about *we*. Value formation takes place in the midst – *in* the relationship."

"We grow when I extend my best relationship-deepening and alliance-improving ideas to others."

"I constantly sense the climate in my alliance and the inner-health of its members. I work to make improvements and help all to grow, have fun and find fulfillment. I focus on *being of value*."

"I am about value. I embody value. *Every* personal interaction is about value – giving, serving, being and loving."

- To others in business we might say:

"**I am the CEO of this alliance** but with *significant differences*."

"Both CEO and alliance manager span the entire lifecycle and the entire business. Both are oriented toward the creation of incremental value for the business."

"However, my decision-making authority and access to resources are limited. So, I primarily depend upon *nontraditional competencies* to accomplish my work."

"I am interested in *all* forms of value – both *tangible* and *intangible*. I have a unique long-term or *timeless* perspective."

"I am primarily responsible for the *enablement* of the alliance's business. Others are primarily responsible for the actual *development* and *delivery* of its business value." (Do not interpret this to mean that alliance managers do nothing. The point is to be clear about our primary focus and the primary focus of others. Primarily we *enable* others to *do*.)

- To family and friends – here is where humility brings us back from our god-like and CEO-like thoughts to simple description, such as:

> "**I am a strategic alliance manager.**"
>
> This does sound impressive, elusive and even a bit mystical. But then others might ask, "What precisely do you *do*?" After repeated questions of clarification from my family, I said:
>
> "**I talk and type …**"
>
> That is how I describe my job to some people. Do we really *do* anything else? But, in fact, the more we actually *do*, the less we enable others' *doings*, and the more we and the alliance will fail. Our success depends upon our empowerment of others.
>
> "**… and think.**"
>
> If we think our job is mostly about *doing*, we should think again. After all, *thinking* is a huge part of our job. We think deeply; we are very thoughtful and mindful.

Are these job descriptions in some ways narcissistic? Not necessarily. These are merely various perspectives on the same truth, perspectives on our core truth, on *who we think we are*.

If you think this section is too bold, reckless or blasphemous, where are those thoughts really coming from? If this section makes you feel a bit uncomfortable because of the pressure it puts on you personally, is that a bad thing?

Think again…

6. The Power in Simple Truths (Solution II – authentic effectiveness)

In this chapter we will deeply explore the intersection of **attitude & mindset** with **relationship,** described in Chapter 4 – *Focus on Personal AND Alliance Success* (see Figure 4.6). Spirituality *defines* that intersection. In fact, spirituality *is* that intersection.[52]

> Spirituality is about deepening relationship –
> with *The Infinite*, with others and with one's Self.

And ... all of these relationships are actually the same relationship.[53] The oneness of these three relationships is empirically true. When we experience a deepening in one of these relationships, the other two relationships deepen, too. As we become more comfortable with our Selves, we have deeper relationships with others. We are more open to spiritual matters and vice versa. These relationships seem to deepen in parallel. As I see it that is what spirituality is about – *deepening relationships.*

This chapter is an extension of Chapter 5, where we started to explore the divine. Toward the end of Chapter 5 we talked about power, specifically the *power* created by *extending our ideas* to others.

This chapter helps us become more effective, in simple ways, by going within.

Simplicity

Simplicity is a subtle, yet empowering, concept in spirituality and in alliancing. Within spirituality, our ability to sense whether we are seeing things simply or complexly can tend to indicate which thought system we are relying upon at that instant.[54] Simplicity leads us toward spiritual truths. Its purpose is to enlighten. Complexity comes from the ego.[55] Its purpose is to obscure the obvious.

Spiritual Principles in Strategic Alliances

In an alliance, complexity clouds our ability to discover hidden insight and opportunity. Thus, complexity impedes value-creation.[56]

The power of simplicity is illustrated in these quotes.

> *Make everything as simple as possible, but not simpler.*
> — A. Einstein

> *All things being equal, the simplest solution tends to be the right one.*
> — Occam's razor

> *Truth is simple. Complexity is of the ego, and is nothing more than the ego's attempt to obscure the obvious.*
> — A Course in Miracles

Simplicity takes us toward truth. We strive for simplicity on the other side of complexity – simplicity based on wisdom and experience.

The Truth

> *Truth can only be known. All of it is equally true, and knowing any part of it is to know all of it.*
> - A Course in Miracles

This chapter suggests five simple truths. They do overlap and they are not easily parsed. The purpose of this book is to be practical, simple and direct. In that spirit, the following statements seem to describe our relationship and experience with truth.

Truth:

- **Works**. We recognize truth by its *results*. We often **see the results in others** before we can see it in ourselves.[57]
- Aligns with and **coalesces** our life **experiences**. Truth *inspires*.

- **Rings true**. Deep within us we *innately recognize* when something is true.
- Seems to be **affiliated with peace**. The more truthful ideas tend to bring us greater peace; and when we are at peace, we tend to see more truthfully. Maybe peace is truth's barometer.

Fundamental Principles

In school I was strongly attracted to physics and calculus.[58] The source of that enthusiasm was the fundamental principles underlying these disciplines.

For the past two decades strategic alliancing has also attracted me. Initially, it was the impressive title; later, the unique breadth of challenges attracted me. Then the attractiveness of the challenge morphed as others described alliance management as a combination of art and science. Perhaps like physics and calculus there are fundamental principles at play in strategic alliances. If so, they should have the same characteristics as other fundamental principles; they should:

- **Lead us toward simplicity**. Simplicity is both the *path* toward truth and a *test* of truth. The simplicity of the wise often sounds naïve and simplistic to the inexperienced.
- **Coalesce prior experiences** and learning. Leading to, "Oh … *now* I understand!"
- Enable **greater problem solving** coupled with **enthusiasm**. Leading to, "Now I can solve *any* problem. Bring it on!"
- **Inspire creativity** and enable an expanded vision – we begin to see a broader range of possibilities.
- Possess **predictive qualities**. We can start "seeing around the corner."
- Illustrate the **interconnectedness** of events – across *time* and *space*. We start seeing with an eternal sense of collective wholeness or the *oneness* of things.

So, what are the fundamental principles in strategic alliance that can start reversing their currently unacceptable failure rates? How can we have greater success? Can we have more fun at the same time? Can we grow to love our work and work our love?

Spirituality – improving attitude & mindset, deepening relationship

To help us transform our alliances, we need a simple definition of spirituaity.

Spirituality is the use of practical principles that deepen relationship.

"*Use*" – thought creates. So "use" means the act of consciously holding certain thoughts in our consciousness. These chosen thoughts will then lead to authentic behaviors. Thus, we "use" them. And, as we use them, we will end up getting used, too (we will be changed).

"*Practical*" – useful *here* and *now*; something that produces an immediate result or benefit. If a solution isn't practical, it isn't spiritual.[59]

"*Principles*" – basic ideas, truths or perspectives, especially our perception of Self, others, the Universe, situations and life. In other words, our **attitude & mindset**.

"*Deepen*" – given our core is divine, deeper is *good*. Given the universal force of love or spirit, going deeper into any relationship is always good. Deeper leads us toward greatness.

"*Relationship*" – with Self, others and the Infinite. That "something" that exists between individuals, companies and organizations. Even *between ideas*. Relationship exists in the midst; it *is* the midst.

The illustration below provides a rich means for talking about spirituality. It sheds light on why this is such an extraordinarily important, yet very difficult, topic to talk about. The metaphor of mankind as fish in water and the water representing spirit provides some practical insights into spirituality. We can see what spirituality *is* and *is not*. We distinguish between *using* versus *debating* spiritual principles. We get a sense of spirit's impact *on* us and *in* us. It helps defuse some of spirituality's mystical aspects. It helps neutralize complexities laid on this topic from some organized religions and spiritual philosophies.

This picture can help us clarify spirituality so we can more openly discuss and ultimately *use* its concepts for practical benefit. Note that if we are *using* water we will ultimately get *used by* water. In our trying to *use* spirit, spirit will *use us*. We will end up being changed. In this process we will be *transformed*.

Figure 6.4 – Spirituality – *using* water (and being *used by* water).

Imagine ourselves as being intelligent fish in an ocean. Water surrounds us and is between us. We are composed of water. We are *in* water and it is *in* us. In fact, we *are* composed of water.

Imagine a school of fish in our little area of the ocean. We may be in this school or we may be observing it. But this school of fish is intensely debating very important issues like:

- The very **existence** of water. If we are *in* water and it is *in* us, how can we *prove* it exists? Being both *comprised of,* as well as *in,* a substance makes it very difficult to prove the existence of that substance.

- We are so close to the water that we are both the **observer** and the **observed**. No wonder it is so hard for us to see it. We have no independent perspective on this substance that is ultimately *us*.
- The true **nature** of water. Does true water have salt or not? Either *your* definition of water or *my* definition of water must be true, but they cannot *both* be true.
- **Experiencing** water. What must we *do* in order to actually experience a state of water-ness? *Where* can we experience true water?
- Being in water's **presence.** What must we do in order to *earn* our right to be in water's presence?
- The **history** and **future** of water. How and when was water created? What is water's future? Where did it come from and where will it go?

We *are* intelligent and thoughtful beings. These are all very interesting and, at times, complex questions. But the questions we *should* be asking are, "Does debating help us *use* water, or is it a distraction? What affect does an understanding of the history or future of water have on our ability to use it, here and now? Does debating help us deepen relationships?" This last question takes us back to something a school or community of fish might practically work on together:

- What *is* **our relationship** with water?
- What are our practical **experiences** with water that we can *share* with one another?
- How can we collectively **grow in our understanding** and *use* of water?

It seems useful to think of the water in this illustration as representing *spirit* or *love*. It is the flow of life force. We can *debate* about water, its substance and flow, or we can *use* water. We can align with the current and more easily travel, or we can fight the flow; we can try to swim upstream.

This "water substance" connects us; we are *in it* and part *of it*. We understand it better when we honestly and openly share our experiences with one another, when we are *in it together*. Because it is in us and we are in it, because it creates a natural oneness, a number of deep principles begin to make sense, such as: we learn by teaching; we are served by serving; we are loved by loving; giving and receiving are one. Our oneness with and because of this stuff makes our life very interesting. Understanding this stuff and using it makes our lives more effective and useful. But it is more helpful when we *share* our experiences about its use with another, rather than debate about it.

Notice other things in this picture. The seahorses symbolize beings who have realized that the purpose of life is to "sing and dance and laugh." And so they help others to sing and dance and laugh.

Also, there is a *flow* of water in this picture. The porpoise has noticed this flow and he chooses to use it. Others can debate water; he uses the flow of water to get somewhere. The porpoise is living a life of purpose!

There is a spiritual jellyfish, a being so like the water, so at one with the water, that we might not notice her. When we are distracted by our complex debating we do not notice such translucent beings. When we start becoming quieter, more present and more aware, we see them and we are amazed by their wisdom and insight. Where did they come from?

If you have observed the illustration above very closely, you might have noticed that one of the large air bubbles has "God" in it, another has "Love" in it. Could it be that "spirit" and "God" and "love" are all words pointing to the same divine substance, of which we are all a part? I share this idea in the spirit of being helpful; this idea seems to help us see each other differently and relate more deeply. I am not sharing this idea to stir up doctrinal debate; simply consider it or discard it based on its usefulness here and now.

This illustration seems to help simplify spirituality so we can focus on *using* it for our practical benefit. It is our choice; we can *use it* or *debate about it*.

Spirituality	
Is	**Is not**
• practically *useful* here and now • about benefits *here* and *now* • *connecting* – deepening relationships – "we" • about *serving*, *healing* and *sharing* • *enthusiastic*, inspirational, insightful, creative • singing, dancing and laughing – being *joyful*	• a theoretical or academic *debate* • about benefits *elsewhere* or *later* • *divisive* – "me vs. you" or "us vs. them" • *depressing*, discouraging • about blame or guilt – being *judgmental* • about preaching, *converting* or "saving"

Table 6.4 – Spirituality *is* and *is not*.

Question: Are We Talking About Religion? Answer: Yes *and* No.

Now the big question, "Are we actually talking about religion?" There are two significant *risks* associated with how we answer this question. And there are two answers to this question.

One risk is premature *rejection* of spiritual ideas, dismissed as "that religious stuff" by those strongly opposed to organized religion. The other risk may actually be more problematic: premature *acceptance*. Someone might assume, "Oh, this is about God. I got it! I already know that stuff." AA's Big Book describes both of these reactions as "contempt prior to investigation." For alcoholics, answering the "religion versus spirituality" question is literally a life and death matter. For alliance managers the risk of prematurely discarding or superficially accepting spiritual ideas can result in continued status quo mediocrity. This is a life and death matter for us as well, but of a different sort. We need to *deeply consider* and ultimately *use* these ideas if they are to make a real difference for us.

Let us get back to the original question, "Are we talking about religion?" "*Yes*," to the degree that religion helps us *use* practical principles *here* and *now* to *deepen relationships*.

Is not religion all deeds and all reflection, and that which is neither deed nor reflection, but a wonder and a surprise ever springing in the soul, even while the hands hew the stone or tend the loom?

— *The Prophet* by Kahlil Gibran

The answer to the question above is "*No*" if religion does not help us deepen relationships here and now. If religious ideas are divisive, lead to debate, take us out of the here and now, or do not deepen relationship, then that it is *not* what we are talking about.

This same question can be asked about philosophy, psychology, self-help books or any other area of personal study. If ideas satisfy the "Is" column of Table 6.4, then the answer is, "Yes – that is what we are talking about; otherwise, no."

If something is not practical, it is not spiritual.

Our practically focused definition of spirituality seems to help. It leads us to the discovery of principles which improve effectiveness in ourselves and in our alliances here and now, not later.

Based on years of study, reflection and practical application, it seems like there are a few simple truths, which are discussed below.[60] There may be other simple truths that you have found to be helpful in your alliancing work, things which help deepen relationships here and now. Please share your experiences.[61]

Remember the power of simplicity. It is interesting when we take philosophical, spiritual or religious ideas to their logical conclusion, to a simple extreme. It is quite interesting.

First, let's think deeply but simply about *thought*.

Two Thought Systems – ego-based or spirit-based, in fear or in love

A common concept in most spiritual teachings is the idea that our greatest struggle is *within* our self (or with our Self). The ancient Greeks talked about having two horses in our heads, one black and one white. Man's day-to-day battle is to determine which horse will take the lead. Spiritual teachings today talk about the ego and spirit as the labels for this inner struggle.[62]

Ego-based thinking promotes a sense of **separateness** – from others, from the Universe, and even from your Self. Separateness breeds a sense of isolation, leading to "me versus you" thinking. The ego-based thought system has a sense of *scarcity*, a need to find fault or judge, the idea of keeping *secrets* and an attraction for *complexity*.[63] *Fear* pervades this thought system. The most damaging fear of all is our fear of success. Intense interactions with others often involve *conflict*, or an attack *of* the other. Competitive comparisons grounded in fear leads to *grandiosity*, to prove that one is better than the other.

Spirit-based thinking promotes a sense of **connectedness** – with others, the Universe and Self. We have an inner-sense of *integrity* or wholeness. We realize that life is "a we thing." Spirit- or love-based thinking brings an awareness of *abundance*. This leads to *openness* and a desire to understand and accept others. Intense interactions are about being *lovingly confrontational*, jointly looking at what is between, what is *in* the relationship, for the *growth* of both parties. Collective and individual greatness embraces *grandeur*. We are *all* grand. And we discover our grandeur *together*.[64]

Spirit-based thinking sees the *simple* essence in things; it sees the truth clearly. Ego-based thinking is biased toward detailed analysis and *complexity*; it is threatened by the truth. The ego uses complexity to obscure its greatest fear, the truth.

Finally, in each decision and in each instant of time, our thoughts are *always* grounded in *one* of these two thought systems. We are either "hostage to the ego" or "host to the spirit and love" – there is no in between.

The Power in Simple Truths

*Would you be hostage to the ego or host to [love]? Let this question be asked ... **every time you make a decision.***

*Every decision you make stems from **what you think you are** and represents the value that you put upon yourself.*
                                            - A Course in Miracles

So as we explore the practical use of five simple truths which deepen relationships, we will look for signs of when we are in *ego* or in *spirit*. When are we in *fear* or in *love*?

Oneness – no separation between people, no duality of thought, integrity

When we hold a sense of oneness in our consciousness, our attitude and behavior toward self and everyone around us authentically changes. And oneness naturally leads to greater honesty and integrity. We increase in power through our integrity and wholeness. Loving service, therefore, makes complete sense, knowing we are ultimately loving our Self.

This table summarizes questions we might ask ourselves to determine whether we have a sense of oneness within ourselves, or if that sense of oneness is absent.

Presence (spirit and love)	Absence (ego and fear)
• Am I treating others as though they *are* me? • Do I realize that what I do to another I am actually doing to myself? • Do I see us as all as being on the same team? Do I see the community among us? • Do I think life is a "we thing?" • Can I hear the collective voice of the entire organization?	• Am I treating another as a separate person? • Do I think that what I do to another has no effect on me? • Do I think my thoughts have no effect on another? (Are there private thoughts?) • Do I view a team as a loose affiliation of individuals, focused solely on self-interests?

Spiritual Principles in Strategic Alliances

Presence (spirit and love)	Absence (ego and fear)
• Do I live a life of wholeness and integrity? • Can I see the interconnectedness of events over time and across space? • Am I focused on our commonalities? • Do I realize that judging is impossible, that I will never know enough to be able to judge? Instead, understanding and accepting are critical.	• Do I think life is a "me versus you" thing? • Do I think that just understanding senior management's view is enough? • Is my life compartmentalized? • Am I oriented toward analyzing situations and events into minute detail? • Do I focus on our differences? • Do I feel it is important to judge? That judging is actually a very useful thing to do so we can find and eliminate faults?

Table 6.7 – Oneness.

Some thought-deepening questions:

- How do universally-accepted truths, such as the Golden Rule or Karma, actually work?[65]

    People simply accept these ideas, but *think about it ... how* do they *actually* work?

    Many consider the Golden Rule as a *suggested* way to treat another, something we *should* do. Could it be that the Golden Rule is also a statement of fact, the *truth about reality*? We *are* one.

- Could it be that what we do to others we are *really* doing *to* ourselves?

- Could it be that how we think and feel toward another is how we are actually thinking and feeling about ourselves?

- How can it be that when we give away our greatest possessions (our ideas, wisdom and love), these things come back to us, with gain?

    How does that *actually* work?

- We often hear that if we want to have loving relationships we need to first love ourselves. Why? And how is self-love actually done?

- If we want to forgive others we must first learn to forgive ourselves. How are these things connected? What does it really mean to forgive? Who are you actually forgiving when you forgive?

- Why does the teacher sometimes learn more than the student? Aside from their rethinking the content of what they're teaching, how is it that the teacher learns when teaching? And *who* are they actually teaching?

- What is the connection between how I view self and how I view others? How are those things actually connected? Why do I attract into my life people whose world view aligns with mine?

- When we change the way we look at things, those things we choose to look at change. How does that actually work?

Now – to be fully present in each instant of time, one eternal now, eternity

It is always best to be more fully present; the more present we are, the better. In such moments creativity emerges and productivity peaks. If we want to affect true positive change in ourselves or in our relationships, we can *only* use the present moment. Feeling bad about the past, feeling guilty or shameful, beating ourselves up for what is not here and now, is self-flagellation – it damages both self and this moment. Bringing up past wrongs in a relationship prevents growth, which can only occur in the present moment. Worrying about the future doesn't help either.

> *The ego regards the present only as a brief transition to the future, in which it brings the past to the future by interpreting the present in past terms.*
>
> — *A Course in Miracles*

Spiritual Principles in Strategic Alliances

Presence (spirit and love)	**Absence** (ego and fear)
• Am I fully present in the here and now? • Is my work like being "in the zone" or "in the flow"? Is my work meditative in nature? • In meetings or conference calls am I honest about being either fully present or gone? • Do I focus on first fully accepting the "is-ness" of a situation? Only after full acceptance do I figure out the next step? • Do I have a timeless perspective? Can I see how the "stars have aligned"? Do I drive toward an end-state vision, coupled with utmost patience and tenacious persistence? • Am I comfortable being alone, in a quiet room, with just my own thoughts?	• What am I thinking? Am I thinking about another time or another place? Where am I? • Am I anxious to be in the next step? Do I think "once XYZ happens, *then* I will be OK"? • Do I live the lie of multi-tasking? Do I think I can check e-mail *and* still be present? • Do I feel like thoroughly examining a bad situation is a waste of time, and immediate action is urgently needed? • Do I have a timed perspective? Do I see the present moment only through the lens of the past, or the future? Am I impatient? Do I over-drive situations? • Do I always need something or someone, like music or white noise, in the background?

Table 6.8 – Now.

Some thought-deepening ideas and questions

- Only in the moment can we really change and truly grow.

- We are most productive, effective and creative when we are in the moment. When we block out any sense of time – time expands and time flies. Why in such timeless moments are we at our very best?

- When we emotionally detach from past problems and future fears, issues tend to resolve themselves.

- Why is meditation effective in increasing creativity and presence? How does that work?

- Does the past exist? Does the future exist? What is time?[66]

"Now" relates to *forgiveness* – to accept – to allow – to give up: Forgiveness undoes the past in the present, releasing the future.

We Are Divine – see the greatness at our core, in everyone, in everything

The Hindu greeting Namasté epitomizes the concept that we are divine:

The god in me sees and rejoices in the god I see in you.

When we choose to see another person as divine, we treat them with great reverence. We see every relationship as sacred and eternal. We recognize the **light** in ourselves and in others. Are we aware of that light? We *are* light.

Presence (spirit and love)	**Absence** (ego and fear)
• Do I see others as being good, trying to do the right thing? • Do I feel that deep down, at my very *core*, that I am good? That *I am great*? That we are all great? There is nothing to fear within. • Do I see us as all indestructible spirits?	• Do I feel like others cannot be trusted? They are "trying to get me." • Am I afraid to go within? Do I think it is dark and scary deep inside? Do I feel like others would run if they really knew me? • Do I feel like survival is precarious, that I am at risk of annihilation? Survival of the fittest.

Table 6.9 – Our Divine Nature.

Some thought-deepening questions:
- Why do relationships fundamentally and authentically improve when we choose to see the greatness in others and then reflect that greatness back to them?
- Is fault-finding *ever* helpful?
- Why is strength-based personal development more effective than weakness-based personal development?[67]

We Create – based on our divine nature, thought is cause

As we become more deeply aware of precisely *what* we are thinking from moment to moment, we will realize the amazing creative power of our thoughts. Of course thought does precede action, but there is more going on here than that. Our thoughts, in and of themselves, directly affect our relationships and they have the power to change our world.

Maybe the admonition of many spiritual teachers to "have a constant prayer in the heart" is not just a suggestion. Maybe it is a statement of reality. Perhaps we *are* always praying or asking. The question is, "What is it that we are always asking for and, in fact, always getting?"

Are we awake or are we making random chaotic requests? Our thought, our attention, *is* our creative **light**. What are we doing with that light?

Presence (spirit and love)	**Absence** (ego and fear)
• Do I recognize that I create "perfectly," based on the thoughts and perspectives I choose to hold? Life *is* a self-fulfilling prophecy, now.	• Do I believe that what I think does *not* matter? Do I believe that the *only* thing that matters is what I *do*?
• Am I "awake" to what I am thinking?	• Am I "asleep," unaware of my thoughts?
• Do I realize that my attention is my "light"? Where and how I choose to focus it causes transcendence, transformation and growth.	• Life is what happens *to* me. We are merely suffering through the "human condition." Life is chaotic, deal with it.
• I choose to see only the good in others and in events. Do I see the good in the world?	• Finding fault is what is most needed. Otherwise, how will others improve?
• Thinking about and pointing out the goodness in everyone and everything leads to greatness.	• Someone needs to point out "areas for improvement." That is my job in life.

Table 6.10 – Thought Creates.

Some thought-deepening questions:

- Some religious teachings suggest we should "have a constant prayer in the heart."[68] Perhaps these are not admonitions for something we should *do*, but instead *a statement of fact*. What if, in reality, we *are always praying*? What if we are *always creating*? And what if our prayers are *always being answered*? Does this change how we think about our thoughts?

- If our thoughts occur without our real awareness, is it any wonder that our lives seem to be out-of-control and chaotic? Are we "asleep at the wheel" of life?

- Do our loving thoughts extend immediately toward others? Do these thoughts affect them, whether they know it or not?[69]

- Have you ever noticed that what you look for, what you deeply expect, ultimately happens? Perhaps not in the form expected; often better than expected.

- Does the idea that you create, here and now, stir up deep fears within you? If so, what are those fears really based on? Is it fear of success?

- Here's an interesting exercise to practice with people in your life. Ask yourself, friends or family members, "What are you thinking *right now*?" Do they really know? Does this question, by itself, deepen relationship by showing your real interest *in* another person? But be ready to hear the truth. It may feel uncomfortable, but it will be good – actually it will be *great*.

- Does this idea expand the ideas in the section titled *Oneness* in Chapter 6? Do we need to be mindful of the thoughts we choose about others? Are they really thoughts directly toward our Self? Does oneness encompass thought?

- What if there are no private thoughts? Does this idea fundamentally change how you think of others?

Love – the universal force which compels growth; enthusiasm, inspiration, joy

We are not talking here about romantic love, but the love that is often equated with God.[70] God *is* love.[71] Love is at the heart of spiritual teachings.[72] Love – the universal force countering entropy.[73] Love compels growth. In my mind love is synonymous with growth. Experience indicates that, in time, all things either grow or die. We as people, organizations, companies, countries and mankind either progress or cease to exist.

In *The Road Less Traveled,* M. Scott Peck defines love as "the will to *extend* oneself for the purpose of nurturing one's own or another's spiritual growth." So, love is equated with *growth,* especially spiritual growth – healthy, loving, positive growth. Spiritual growth is rooted in love.

> *"Teach only love, for that is what you are." This is the one lesson that is perfectly unified, because it is the only lesson that is one. Only by teaching it can you learn it. "As you teach, so will you learn." If that is true, and it is true indeed, do not forget that what you teach is teaching you.*
>
> *- A Course in Miracles*

Presence (spirit and love)	**Absence** (ego and fear)
• Do I recognize the love within me? Can I accept my greatness, my grandeur, in humility? • Do I experience this love among us and between us (like the water in Figure 6.4)? • No matter what, things will ultimately work out for the best. Am I optimistic? • Do I live a life of acceptance?	• Am I in fear? Fear of failure. Mostly fearful of success. Fear of my grandeur. • Am I afraid of others? Am I fearful of life's events? • Is my outlook basically pessimistic? Fear, worry, depression, sadness, anger. • Am I judgmental? • Do I have a sense of separation?

Presence (spirit and love)	**Absence** (ego and fear)
• Do I have a sense of connectedness? • Am I self-assured? For example, in negotiating, can no deal actually be the best deal? • A belief that the best growth comes from focusing on the good and strengths. I can then simply *let* growth happen.	• Survival mode? Is every deal a must-win deal to assure my personal survival. • A belief that growth only really comes from focusing on problems, mistakes and weaknesses. I must *make* growth happen.

Table 6.11 – Love.

Some thought-deepening questions:

- Do we clearly see what is happening around, within and among us?

- Does an optimistic outlook, a deep-seated belief that growth is inevitable, always produce better results?

- What is the interconnecting "stuff" between people, organizations, companies, countries and even between ideas? How are these things actually interconnected? What is the substance of those connections?

- Could it be that as loving thoughts are extended, *love* forms the connectedness *between* us?

- Is love "that wordless language of empathy," creating an atmosphere in which we can "feel time, touch reality and recognize spiritual values long lost"?[74]

- Could it be that our loveless, fearful thoughts cannot be extended, so they end up being *projected* onto others?

- Are we all naturally biased toward love?

Assessing and Changing Attitude & Mindset

So, as we are working with others, as we are *thinking* about others, as we are *thinking* about ourselves, as we are *thinking* about our alliance, we ask ourselves, "What is my currently-chosen *perspective*?"

> Can I *hear* the voice of the collective?
> Do I *see* others as myself? ....**Oneness**
> Am I *fully present*, in this instant of time,
> *here* and *now*? ....**Now**
> Can I *see*: the *divine* in all,
> all relationships as *sacred* and *eternal*? ....**We are Divine**
> Do I *see* my loving thoughts as *light*?
> Am I *mindful* of my thoughts? ....**We Create**
> Am I *optimistic*? Do I see *goodness* as
> inevitable? Am I *in love*? ....**Love**

Assessing and changing our own attitude & mindset sounds simple. But this is extraordinarily hard work, it requires persistence, patience, self-love and healthy relationships with trusted others. Beyond sounding simple and being hard, this is *our most important work*. This work is at the heart of transformation.[75] This is how we as individuals will "be the change" *in* our strategic alliance. This is how we will live with great integrity, loving our work and working our love – not as a workaholic but as an enthused transformational change agent.

Sustained spiritual growth encompasses certain characteristics:

1. **This work is best/only done with trusted others – life is a "we thing."** We may *think* we know what is going on inside us, but often we do not. When we struggle with problematic situations, when we are stressed out, we need trusted others. We each need an interpersonal "strategic alliance." We need confidants with whom we can have open, trustful and in-depth discussions. We need people who will tell us the truth as they see it, based on their own personal experiences and what they see in us, not based on prescribed practices or dogma. We need others, trusted others, who can be objective "sounding boards," where we can "get things out" without

the fear of being judged. We need relationships where we can fearlessly and thoroughly examine our own hypocrisies, where we can embrace our hypocrisies.

We need an environment where the focus is on what is *between* us, not on any one person. A setting where the discussion is based on shared experiences. Where it is not about "fixing" someone else or having someone "fix" us. Where it is not about debating and proving someone is wrong so the other can be right. We need a place where we are all about teaching, learning, sharing, healing and loving together, as a community. We need a place where we can learn *to use practical spiritual principles*. This type of practical growth occurs *in between* – in between people and within ourselves.[76]

2. **This work is all-encompassing.**

If we are about living a life of integrity and wholeness we can expect to gain insights in one area of our life and apply them in other areas.

> *When the student is ready the teacher will appear.*
> *When the teacher is ready the student will appear.*
> *And when the student is really ready he will realize*
> *The teacher is with him* always *and* everywhere.

There are limitless opportunities in our life where we can have learning/teaching opportunities and draw closer to the truth within and between us:

- Working with a trusted manager, personal coaches, clergy, psychiatrists and psychologists.
- Personal inventories like MMPI (psychiatric assessments), or **www.strengthsfinder.com** (focusing on strengths), 4th Step work in 12-step recovery (assessing personal defects and assets), personality assessments – this work is about first accepting and then embracing (growing through) personal hypocrisy or integrity gaps.

- Working in 12-step recovery programs, support groups and trust-filled communities.
- In-depth discussions with dear friends, life companions, family members, colleagues and co-workers.
- Anyone, anywhere, anytime – constantly and openly solicit feedback from others, as appropriate – deeply listen to the Universe.

A while back I was with my oldest son at my barber. My barber and I were having a deep discussion about our personal spiritual experiences. Afterward, my son asked me, "Is there anyone you do *not* have these types of discussions with?" To which I said, "I certainly hope not."

3. **This work calls for – and so it develops – openness and fearlessness**. This work requires great love – confidence that growth will occur and things will improve over time. It requires us to face our fears – the fear of going within, fear of failure and, most deeply, our fear of success.

All this stuff – trust, love, openness, fearlessness – seem to go together. These things develop and deepen together. Relationships with self, others, and spirit/God/Universe seem to deepen in parallel.

Below are two paragraphs from the book *A Return to Love* by Marianne Williamson. You may have previously heard the first paragraph; it is quoted in a couple of movies (it is incorrectly attributed to Nelson Mandela):

> *Our deepest fear is not that we are inadequate. Our deepest fear is that we are powerful beyond measure. It is our light, not our darkness that most frightens us. We ask ourselves, Who am I to be brilliant, gorgeous, talented, fabulous? Actually, who are you not to be? You are a child of God. Your playing small does not serve the world. There is nothing enlightened about shrinking so that other people won't feel insecure around you. We are all meant to shine, as children do. We were born to make manifest the glory of God that is within us. It is not just in some*

of us; it is in everyone. And as we let our own light shine, we unconsciously give other people permission to do the same. As we are liberated from our own fear, our presence automatically liberates others.

4. **This work leads to an amazingly fulfilling life.** Fasten your seat belt! Is there more important work?

   A miracle worker is an artist of the soul. There's no higher art than living a good life. An artist informs the world of what's available behind the masks we all wear. That's what we're all here to do. The reason so many of us are obsessed with becoming stars is because we're not yet starring in our own lives. The cosmic spotlight isn't pointed at you; it radiates from within you. I used to feel like I was waiting for someone to discover me, to 'produce' me, like Lana Turner at the drugstore. Ultimately I realized that the person I was waiting for was myself. If we wait for the world's permission to shine, we will never receive it. The ego doesn't give that permission. Only God does, and He has already done so. He has sent you here as His personal representative and is asking you to channel His love into the world. Are you waiting for a more important job? There isn't one.

5. **The work is ongoing, ever-deepening and ever-expanding.** At the start of each work day, decide ahead of time what kind of day you want to create. Decide what thought system you will consciously use as you make decisions throughout the day.[77]

Who will be helping you make decisions, ego or spirit? How will you be able to distinguish which thought system you are using at any point in time for any specific decision? Are there trusted others you can check in with as needed, for a "sanity check?" Are there people to help you see more clearly what thought system you are relying on? With whom can you confide to accurately assess your motives?

Ego is based on separation and fear, leading to projection

and a need to "*make* things happen." Spirit is based on connectedness, peace and love, leading to extension of ideas and *creating*.

When things seem distressing, take a break, take a breath.[78] Do we want to be right or at peace? Perhaps there is another perspective. Do we want to judge or accept?

Summon the courage to live a life beyond your wildest dreams!

Seek the path of the soul and let your spirit show you the way.
Embrace the truth as you would a beloved friend,
and revel in the freedom that she brings.
View the world through loving eyes that see
goodness and beauty all around.
Practice the art of seeing with
your eyes closed and your mind open.
Summon the courage to paint your own destiny.

— Sally Deems-Mogyordy

7. The Value of Spirituality in Business Relationships (Impact)

In this chapter we will diverge from the book's flow; but first, let's do a quick recap of what we've covered.

Earlier in the book we presented compelling arguments for the strategic *need* for spirituality in alliancing work. We've looked at the root cause for alliance *failures* and the often onerous *challenges* we face. Then we flipped things around by looking at the overlap of personal *and* alliance *success*. We then deeply and profoundly explored the *role* of alliance manager from unique and *empowering* perspectives. In the last chapter, we suggested some spiritual *principles* or *ideas* we can hold in consciousness that will have the natural result of authentically affecting our *behavior* in positive ways.

So far this book hasn't asked for you to *do* much of anything, just change your attitude & mindset, and change your thoughts. Before we get into *practices* or what you might *do*, it is important to provide some rationale for *why* you should invest your time and energy into *using* spiritual practices in your alliance work. This is especially important, given some of the practices suggested in Chapter 8 will be *nontraditional* and *counterintuitive*.

So *why* change? What's in it for me? What's in it for the business? Spirituality transforms us and our alliances, but it *is* hard work. We take risks and we face deep-seated fears when we try to bring spiritual principles into our work. We do need answers to these questions.

The purpose of this section is to answer the question, "Why change?"

Personal Value

Why should you, a strategic alliance manager, invest your limited time and energy into using spiritual principles at work? This spiritual stuff is often hard work. You will have to deal with fears, both yours and others. What is your personal return-on-investment for spirituality? Listed below are personal benefits, attributes which will develop *in* you:

- **Naturally Connected** – part of

    Through simple spiritual acts, such as meditation, mindfulness, presence and awareness, we connect with Self, others and the Universe. We are at ease with our Selves and with others. Whether we are in a large gathering or all alone, we are not lonely. We feel comfortable in our own skin. We are at *peace*. There is a certain ease others experience in our presence. This helps us authentically connect, which naturally fosters deep relationships.

- **A Practical Visionary** – a seer

    As we meditate and become more comfortable in the quiet presence of our Selves, we gain insight. We realize that there is something intrinsically powerful and wise at our core. Some spiritual teachers say that, given we are children of God and God is love, we must be love, too – at our core we are love. When we connect with our insightful wisdom coupled with love, it cannot help but inspire and enthuse us and others.

    In quiet moments of reflection and meditation, we receive answers to our most vexing problems. As we deeply connect with the collective of the alliance, we gain *a vision of possibility*. As alliance managers we are grounded in the practicalities of business. Thus, we can become practical visionaries, visionaries with our feet planted firmly on the ground. Our alliances are "where the rubber meets the blue sky" – where visions and dreams are realized *together*.

- **Greater Integrity** – wholeness

    We achieve great wholeness as we confront and heal personal integrity gaps or hypocrisies. We increase in personal power as we align our thoughts, beliefs and actions. We no longer have anything to hide. We realize the value in confronting, rather than avoiding, issues. This leads to greater *wholeness in life,* as we "love our work, work our love and live with devotion."

- **Deeply Principled** – doing what's right

When we connect to and live from the truth within us, we are no longer living with the result of other's thinking. As Steve Jobs said, we are no longer trapped by dogma.[79] We *intrinsically know* what the next right thing is for all concerned. Often our unique insight causes us to take on difficult issues; our internal grounding makes this both possible and necessary. Highly ethical and principle-driven results naturally occur for us and our alliance.

- **Peacefully at One** – at one in the midst

The simple idea that we are one, all on the same team, starts to become intuitively obvious. Subsequently, we realize that individual and collective success occur together. This is how true greatness is achieved. We become more committed to the success of others and the alliance at large than to our own individual success. Paradoxically, this will end up bringing us great personal success; and more importantly, it will bring us joy and peace.

When we are in a state of peacefulness, strong emotions do not scare us. We become increasingly comfortable receiving and expressing intense emotions. Our peaceful presence allows us to deal with difficult issues in relationships. Our growing peacefulness allows us to be comfortable and adaptive in the midst of the chaos that is often present in and around our alliance. We are okay being in "the eye of the hurricane."

We realize that *spirit lives in the collective*, in the midst of our alliance. As we tune in, as we pay attention to the collective as a whole, we hear a voice speak to us. In spiritual matters, words often fail us; in this situation, we realize that *voice* is also *light*. The voice of the collective is shared light. The light of the spirit in the midst neutralizes issues and reveals opportunities. This light helps us rise above issues what would have constrained us; light has *transcendental* properties. It is also *transformational*; it changes problems into insights and clears the way to find new opportunities. There is real power when we do our work by this shared light that lives in our midst.

If we are, in fact, one, then giving and receiving is one thing. When we give of our self to another, we are actually giving *to* our Self. In alliancing I have tested out a counterintuitive and arguably dangerous act I call "self-obsolescence." If I strive to give to you my wisest ideas, if I try to make it so you no longer *need* me, mystical things start happening: you have a natural compulsion to give back; and so as I gain wisdom, and as you start *wanting* me, rather than needing me, my virtual presence naturally expands. As I empower you, you end up empowering me; and between us we create a *virtuous cycle of growth and love*. In the midst of the process of self-obsolescence, I end up obsoleting my lesser self for my greater Self, and we all gain power.[80] Such is the power that lives in empowerment.

- **Co-fronting Difficult Issues** – loving confrontation

With awareness and loving presence we can bring up difficult issues and take the resultant discussion to a positive outcome. We practice loving confrontation as we stay mindful of our oneness. I find it helpful to repeat a definition of Namasté when I am in a difficult conversation: "The god in me sees and rejoices in the god I see in you." This reminds me that the person I am with is *divine* and that our relationship is *eternal*; this is *a transformational perspective*. Loving confrontation differs from conflict. The former is about *co-fronting* (or co-facing) difficult issues *in* a relationship, and the latter is about attacking another person. Given the reality of our oneness, loving confrontation makes absolute sense, and conflict makes no sense at all; conflict is, in fact, insane.

Over time we may actually learn to enthusiastically *embrace hypocrisies and shadows* – ours and our alliances'. We learn that by collaboratively facing (co-fronting) challenges in our alliance, we discover new insights and we uncover previously unseen opportunities. These insights and opportunities are hidden by personal hypocrisies and organizational shadows. Until a problematic situation (a shadow) is thoroughly acknowledged and fearlessly accepted, the window of opportunity remains shut and we stagnate; mediocrity prevails.[81] However, with a loving perspective grounded in oneness, loving confrontation ends up becoming a fulfilling game of "hide and seek" – *shadows hide* valuable things, and our *shared light illuminates* them.

- **Entrusted with Trust** – trustworthy

    A counterintuitive thing happens when we bring loving confrontation into a relationship; trust actually comes shortly thereafter. Loving confrontation *calls for* trust, and so trust comes; trust is a result of growth-oriented (loving) confrontation. So, as we deal with difficult issues and find insights and opportunities, trust will grow in our alliance. And given that trust is *the* issue in any relationship, our alliance will stay on path toward greatness.

- **An Illuminating Mirror** – grateful and appreciative

    As we come to understand the power of our light and the reality of oneness, we naturally tap into the astounding power of *gratitude* and *appreciation*. Just as we have a hard time seeing our own shortcomings, we also cannot clearly see our assets; we need each other's light for this. When we are grateful and express appreciation, we use our light, our attention, to *see the greatness in another* person or in another company, and we reflect their greatness back to them.

    As I see it, gratitude is the most powerful form of communication. Gaining an ability to authentically and powerfully express deeply impactful gratitude will have the effect of drawing our alliance together and inspiring us toward collective grandeur.

Gratitude is the paddle we use in the river of life to draw us closer to one another and align ourselves with Divine Will.

We cannot say too much about the power of gratitude, the power in being an illuminating mirror to another.

- **A Creative Creator** – full creative expression

    Our Creator created us to create. As we tap into the source of truth and light within us, as we use the transformational power of shared light in the midst of our alliance, as we openly listen to the voice of the collective in our alliance, we will become increasingly inspired. Great ideas will just come to us. And people throughout our alliance will seek us out for our creative influence.

- **The Metaphor for Metamorphosis** – be the change

    We will see things others cannot or will not see. We will become increasingly aware of the needs in our alliance. We will begin to understand Gandhi's adage, "You must *be* the change you want to *see* in your world." As we see deficiencies in our alliance, we will first go within ourselves and ask how well we are living with that issue; we will embrace our own hypocrisies, knowing that's how growth (love) begins.

    We will work to emulate the positive changes we wish to see in our alliance. If the atmosphere is one of scarcity and fear, we will strive to live with abundance and love. If there is a lack of trust, we will strive to be worthy of trust. We become the metaphor or symbol for the metamorphosis or change needed in our alliance – it has to start within *us*.

- **A True Servant-Leader** – an authentic giver

    Servant-leaders lead by serving and giving. That's actually all we have been talking about so far. Servant-leadership is a natural result of the embodiment of spiritual principles. Now it becomes easy, natural and authentic. All we really want to do is serve because we know it comes back to us. We serve and love and give, not because we are selfless, but because we are selfish in the truest way; we are Self-full – full of Self.

- **Full of One's Self** – greatest experience of Self

    You will acquire a true sense of Self – true humility and true pride. You will gain a greater inborn level of confidence – not arrogance or grandiosity – but *assertive grandeur*. You will become full of Self. This Self, your innate grandeur, realizes you cannot do this alone: life and your alliance is all a "we thing."

- **Productive Community** – attract success home

    Increased effectiveness throughout the alliance is achieved indirectly via subtle but powerful nontraditional means. We establish a pervasive virtual presence throughout the alliance. We attract success and success-filled people.

    Our alliance becomes a productivity community, a place where people come and feel *at home*. This will occur as your alliance's timeless value-creating vision starts becoming realized. It is a lovingly-intense place where high trust allows constructive (loving) confrontation to easily occur. This home is not about fault-finding; it is about developing and extending our collective greatness. In such a place collective good and individual good are *one*. We become collectively and individually empowered as fears are faced, transcended and even embraced.

    While this home is stable in its love, there is a sense of *bounded instability*, or order at the edge of *chaos*. In such a place new opportunities naturally surface and are quickly assessed and developed. Given our alliance is becoming a catalyst for value-enabling growth, it may end up constructively disrupting our own company.

    With its clear vision, collective persistence and tenacity become the norm; "*no* is simply not yet yes." We lovingly push through impediments to realize greater value. We regularly do the impossible.

- Legendary – leave a legacy

    What you will achieve in your alliance will become the thing of legends. Your alliance will accomplish an impressive and inspiring legacy that will forever move beyond status quo mediocrity. And you will realize that you could not have done this alone. As in life, alliancing is very much a "we thing."

Does this sound like it would be helpful for you and your alliance?

The ROI of Spirituality in Strategic Alliances

Why should management care if their alliance managers use spiritual principles or not? What is the company's return-of-investment for the practical use of spiritual principles?

- **One-third of corporate revenue** is tied to alliances and partner relationships.[82] And this trend is increasing exponentially at a rate of 25% growth each year.

- **57% of alliances fail** to achieve their expected results.[83]

- **40% of alliance failure** is due to **relationship**: low trust, ineffective collaboration, poor communication, etc.

- **Spirituality** is the use of **simple principles** that make behavior more authentic. Spirituality deepens and **improves relationships**, thus enabling both greater value-discovery *and* value-creation.

- Let's assume that the practical use of spiritual principles had only a **25% impact on relationship-caused failures**. This would result in relationship issues causing 30% of the failures, rather than 40% of the failures today. This would lead to a **5% increase in alliance success rate**. So 52% of alliances would fail, rather than 57% today.[84]

- Given one-third of corporate revenue is tied to business relationships, a 5% increase in alliance success rate could lead to a **1.5-2% growth in overall revenue**. For a billion dollar organization this would equate to **$15-20 million dollars** in increased revenue. If your corporation's revenue could increase by 1.5-2%, would the use of spirituality in alliances be worth it?

Using spiritual principles to change attitude & mindset and deepen relationship significantly impacts business. We start by transforming ourselves and our alliance.

Alliance Climate Change

Be the change you want to see in the world.
- Mahatma Gandhi

What impact can just one person have on an alliance's overall climate? History is full of examples where just one person made a huge difference – for a country and for all of mankind. Consider the impact these individuals have had: Mahatma Gandhi, Jesus Christ, Dalai Lama, Albert Einstein, Abraham, Buddha, Martin Luther King and *You* (Time Magazine's Person of the Year in 2006).

As we go within and embrace our personal hypocrisies or integrity gaps, we become empowered and emboldened to confront trust and integrity issues in our alliance. As we increasingly trust ourselves, trust will also grow in our world around us. Trust is <u>the</u> foundation of any relationship and is critically important in long-term value-creating alliances. Improving trust will create a healthier climate in our alliance.

We have the opportunity to lead the transformation of our alliance team to becoming a productive community, a place where value-creating vision is clearly seen and inevitably achieved. In this community, in this home, healthy confrontation becomes the norm for the collective good. Individuals *and* the community grow and succeed. This transformation is both "*all about us* and *nothing about us.*"

The alliance will have a positive impact on the broader organization within both companies. For the good of the overall business, the alliance will at times disrupt a company's norms, procedures and systems. The nontraditional competencies of relationship developed in an alliance will naturally spread throughout each company, increasing the effectiveness of all collaboration, both internal and external.

Business Transformation

Organizational learning from our alliance will benefit other intercompany relationships and other areas of a business. Relationship-deepening and alliance-oriented competencies that work in an alliance will work in other places. Such competencies include:[85]

- Improved **listening** skills and interpersonal **rapport** building – create stronger and more effective teams. Greater trust leads to more open communication.

- Accelerating the **surfacing and resolution of problematic situations** and **differences**. These problems are first accepted, then transcended and finally transformed. Things are more immediately dealt with, not avoided. More than just being "dealt with" or managed, these problems are transformed into new business opportunities.

- Treating **relationship as a corporate asset**, worth assessing and developing in and of itself.

- The ability to consider and measure a **broadened range of value** – especially *intangible* and *longer*-term forms, ultimately leading to better long-term growth.

- A more **service-oriented** mindset – *giving to receive* – for the greater good. Show how to move beyond selfish-interests toward *self-full* interests.

- Greater **creativity** – better and more broadly shared ideas.

- **Timelessness** of perspective – the ability to see trends and connect the dots – increased **patience**, **persistence** and **presence**.

The fear-based, zero-sum-game of "me vs. you" or "your win is my loss" mindset in business has run its course. Maniacally competitive environments are stifling business' ability to create new value. This climate is stifling and oppressive for the people and for the business. There is a better way to live and flourish.

The Value of Spirituality in Business Relationships

What is business without people? The oppression we often feel in the world of business is within and without, within and between people, within and between businesses and customers.

As alliances transcend the unhealthy, value-limiting constraints of their past, they will help the broader business transform, too. This will not undermine competitiveness, but it will transform the notion of competition into a higher comparative form. Rather than individuals and companies thinking, "I want to be better than you so I can beat you," they will start thinking:

> *The greatness I see in you inspires me to greatness – as a person and as a company.*

What will the world of business be like when "I am going to kick your ass" gets transformed into "You make me want to be a better person"? Will it be more or less intense?[86] Will it be more or less valuable, more or less able to create value?

Is this being Pollyannaish? I certainly hope so! Pollyanna was just one person who changed the world around her.

Alliance Managers – spearheads of collaborative growth

There is a phrase from the *Big Book* of Alcoholics Anonymous that captures our broadest vision as alliance managers – our potential impact for greatness in the world of business. Imagine ourselves as "intelligent agents, spearheads of God's ever-advancing Creation."[87] At our best we are transformational change agents helping others see and achieve our collective grandeur.

We are trailblazers. We can help others in our alliance "get it," in terms of the value *in* relationship and in terms of how to collaborate better to enable greater value-creation. We can help others throughout business "get it." We can also help others in other areas of our lives "get it." We embody practical, spiritually-based principles, refined in the intense proving-ground of strategic alliancing. We understand the nontraditional competencies needed to improve collaboration like no one else. The positive changes we make within ourselves will transform our alliances, which will help businesses become more conscious. Ultimately, we can transform the world. This is how important our job is!

8. Some Spiritual Practices in Strategic Alliancing (Solution III)

In Chapter 7 we presented real-world motivation (ROI) for the practical use of spirituality, for ourselves, for our alliances, and for our companies. With that motivation we now suggest some spiritual *practices* – things an alliance manager might *do*. If you have additional or different perspectives on some of these ideas, we would love to hear from you.[88]

These practices *will* change attitude & mindset – ours and others'. The result *will* be deepened relationships and, therefore, greater value-creation. Some of these ideas may sound simple, but the work can be quite hard; putting them into practice calls for persistence and tenacity. This work is best be done with trusted others; therefore, these practices call for and create trust. Some of these practices overlap with other practices. Mutual exclusivity is impossible to achieve because we are using simple truths, and truth cannot be neatly parsed into discrete non-overlapping pieces.

Starting with the basics, we progress into ever-deeper spiritual practices. For each practice we cover five topics: situation, basic ideas, practical steps, spiritual basis and benefits.

Fasten your seat belt …

Presence – mindfulness, the lie of multi-tasking, be present or be gone

This practice is about the *power of presence*, being truly in the moment. Situations *always* improve with greater presence. If for some reason you choose not to be present, be honest – you are gone.

Presence – *Situation*

Businesses increasingly expect us to multi-task. We must be always-on and always-available. Our attention is stretched so thin that it is impossible to truly answer the question, "Where am I?" If we believe we can truly multi-task and be many places at once, we are, in fact, nowhere. We are definitely not present.

Is multi-tasking *always* the right thing - for us and for business?

When we are not mindfully present in a meeting, how should we respond when someone "blindsides" us with a question that we cannot answer *because* we are not present?[89]

Presence – *Basic Ideas*

Things *always* work out better when we are *fully present*. This is a bold statement. Can you think of any exception? This is not to say that we should not receive calls during meetings. But it *is* to say that we should always *strive* to be fully present. When you are receiving a call, for example, be fully present in that conversation. Be honestly present, always, everywhere and with everyone.

When we are totally immersed in an activity, we are "in the zone" or "in the flow."[90] Creativity is optimized. We are enthused by the task. We lose track of time. We are aligned with the flow of life.

By being fully present in meetings, we do not miss out on what is going on. We make great contributions to the team's work. We are more aware of the important subtleties in the environment, all of which are critically important in an alliance. We sense the alliance's climate.

Do not underestimate the subtlety of presence. It is very easy to assume we are present when we are not. Constantly ask, "What am I thinking? Where am I?"

Be honest. If you are not present in a meeting and you are asked a question you are not prepared for, be truthful and say, "Sorry, I *was not here*. I was somewhere else. Can you repeat that question?" Respect the divine in all relationships. Have clear honesty in your thoughts. Admit it if you are not present.

Presence – *Practical Steps*

1. Practice the art of *being*. On a regular basis practice quieting the mind or meditation in some form.[91]

Some Spiritual Practices in Strategic Alliancing

All of man's miseries derive from not being able to sit quietly in a room alone.

— Blaise Pascal – French scientist, mathematician and philosopher

2. Be *aware* of what you are thinking. Observe your thoughts. You will then be more present.
3. Ask yourself, *"Where am I?"* Am I present, right here? Or am I wishing I were somewhere else? Am I thinking about the past or the future? Is my attention focused on *here* and *now*?
4. Am I *multi-tasking* in a meeting? If so, am I honest with myself and with others about my lack of presence? Will I honestly admit my lack of presence if someone asks me a question?

Presence – *Spiritual Basis*

- **Now** – respect each instant of time. Neither the past nor the future exists. "Now" is the closest we will get to eternity in this world. One eternal now.
- **We create** – those things upon which we focus our attention grow. Growth only occurs *here* and *now*.
- **We are divine** – be respectful of others – relationships among the divine are sacred and eternal.
- **Love** – lack of presence is caused by, and causes, fear. Choose instead to be "in love." Know that growth is inevitable. Growth is simply a matter of time.

Presence – *Benefits*

- Presence establishes a solid **foundation** for continued **spiritual growth**, like awareness.
- Greater presence increases **creativity and productivity**, both

individually and collectively.

- There is greater **honesty**. We are either present or we are not. We are honest with ourselves and others about our state-of-presence. This bold honesty puts the "spotlight" on the idea of presence.

- **Climate improves** in the alliance. Our presence and the presence of others increase. Collective awareness of the environment increases. Corrective action logically follows from this awareness.

- **Trust, the foundation in relationships, improves** with an honest, healthy change in climate.

Awareness – listen holistically, listen to the collective, see the flow

Once you are truly *present*, you can develop and deepen *awareness*. We become *aware* by observing what is truly going on within us and around us. Often what is going on within us is a mirror of what is going on around us, and vice versa; we notice this connection when we are increasingly aware. *Listening* based on awareness becomes deeper and more intense. Such listening can help us become confrontational in a loving way.[92] Awareness is noticing the interconnected flow of life's events occurring around us.

Awareness – *Situation*

In Chapters 2 and 3 we discussed the intensity, complexity and drama in strategic alliances. Simultaneously, alliance managers are being drawn to multi-task; always-on pressures mount. There is so much happening in our world that we become oblivious to what is *really* happening *in* our surroundings. Sensory overload makes us numb; we lose awareness.

Where there is distraction, listening is impossible. When we do not *listen*, we do not *understand*; as a result, *communication* is impossible. Without an understanding of our audience, we may as well be "talking to the void." As an alliance manager, we need to *understand* our alliance if we are to *manage* it. Otherwise, we may as well be "managing the void."

What *is* going on around us?

Awareness – *Basic Ideas*

One of our most important relationship-building skills is *listening*. The more we understand each other, the more effective are our negotiations and the better our outcomes. Such understanding depends upon our ability to listen. Business people speak of the need for *active* listening. However, consider the paraphrase below from *The Power of Now*, which describes a deeper level of listening beyond active – *holistic listening*:

> *When listening to another person, don't just listen with your mind, listen with your whole body. Feel the energy as you listen. This form of listening creates a still space that enables you to truly listen, giving the other person space – a space to be. This space to be is the most precious gift you can give. Pay attention to the Being of the other person underneath the words and underneath the mind. This listening creates a clear space of no-mind within which the relationship flowers.*[93]

We need to actively, deeply and holistically *listen* to the people in our alliance. An alliance contains *many* people. Surrounding all of these people is the alliance's *environment*. We grow in our understanding of the alliance as we truly listen to as many people as possible at all levels of management and in all functional areas. We then *coalesce* what we hear into a collective statement *from* the alliance. From collective listening and deep hearing we can then understand the alliance's *environment*. This is awareness – collectively listening to the people and sensing the environment.[94]

Listening *to* the collective results in a deeper awareness. Look again at Figure 6.4, Spirituality – *using* the water. Consider the *flow* of that water. As we extend our awareness throughout our alliance, we begin to sense a subtle, yet powerful, *flow*. This flow affects the environment, which then impacts people and events.[95] As our awareness of this flow increases, we are presented with a choice. We can choose to *align* with that flow or we can *fight* it. With *alignment* we *surrender* – not by giving *up*, but giving *in* – surrendering to win and winning more.

This concept is deep. Be patient. Give yourself some time and some practice. Read on.

As we increase our awareness of flow, our awareness of *time* also changes. A few years ago I experienced such a changed awareness. I had to acquire a *timeless* or time-compressed perspective. Figure 8.2 shows how events involving six companies over six years had to occur before HP could establish an alliance with SAP. In 2003, I had to look back four years, see how seemingly disparate events were actually interconnected, and then see how the flow of this collective momentum could be used for HP's benefit. It then took two more years for HP to capitalize on this multi-company, multi-year momentum. Two years sounds like a long time, but in the area of enterprise software, where product lifecycles are measured in decades, two years is relatively quick.[96]

Here is a synopsis of the six years of interconnected events. In 1999, HP acquired Dazel. This led to early discussions between HP and SAP, but SAP was not yet ready to "open up" their original equipment manufacturer (OEM) strategy.[97] It took five more years before SAP became ready. First SAP had to acquire TopTier, and Adobe had to acquire Acellio. Then Adobe had to convince SAP to be willing to OEM Adobe's software and integrate it into SAP NetWeaver.[98] Next, in 2003, HP established an alliance with Adobe to co-market solutions to SAP's customers and help HP better understand and deeply influence SAP. Two years later, in 2005, the "stars aligned" and HP established its co-development and co-marketing alliance with SAP. It was simply a matter of time.

Some Spiritual Practices in Strategic Alliancing

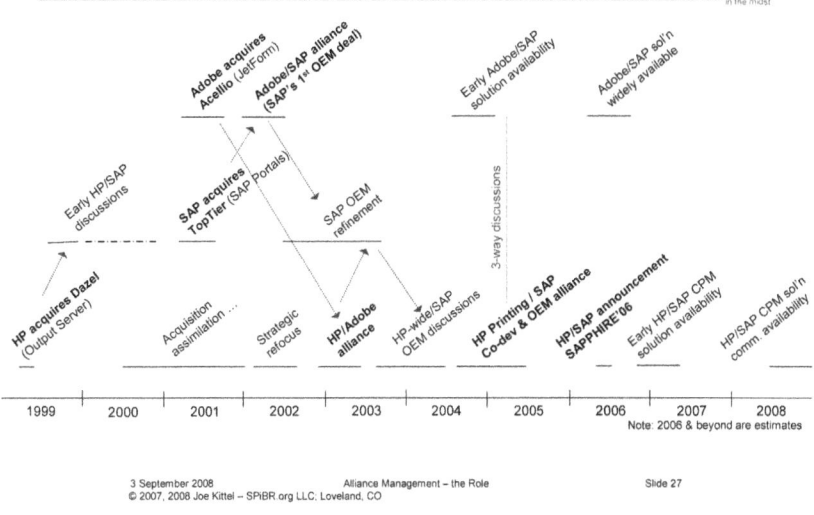

Figure 8.2 – Timeless Awareness.

This alliance happened because we were able to span across six years and acquire a *timeless awareness* of events. This *timelessness of perspective* provided us with patience and persistence. Organizational patience was sorely needed during 18 months of executive level discussion, including nine months of contractual negotiations. With our acquired timeless awareness we saw the inevitable and knew a deal was "simply a matter of time." This $300 million relationship was announced by HP and SAP in May of 2006.[99] Today the overall HP/SAP enterprise printing alliance is valued in excess of a billion dollars per year.

Awareness – *Practical Steps*

1. When talking with another person, focus your attention totally on that other person. Then shift slightly and focus your attention *in* that other person. Be totally *present*. Feel what they are saying. Hear what they are not saying.

2. Listen *holistically* with your entire being, allowing the other

person the openness to *be*.

3. Listen to the alliance by having in-depth and substantive *listening* sessions with as many people as possible. Be aware of the environment or climate in the alliance.[100]

4. *Take the time* to *step back* and see events from a *timeless* and a *space-less* perspective.[101]

   a. See how events are playing out over time.
   b. Look into the past as well as into the future. See the flow.
   c. Notice how events affect various companies or various organizations within your own company. See things evolve in a holistic manner.
   d. See trends occurring over time, indicating a certain direction or flow of events.
   e. Connect events within and outside of the alliance and see how things are flowing in the ecosystem and industry.

5. Be aware of what is going on *all around you*, in the broadest possible sense. Continually work to *expand*, *extend* and *deepen* your awareness.

Awareness – *Spiritual Basis*

- **We are divine** – all relationships among divine beings are sacred. Stay constantly aware of this truth.
- **Now** – do not allow time (past or future) to distract you from your awareness of what is happening here and now. Yet, also see the timelessness of events occurring within companies, across ecosystems, throughout industries and in the global economy. See the flow.
- **Oneness** – listen to others, individually and collectively. Listen as though you are listening to yourself; in many ways you are. Be open to seeing oneness across time and across space.
- **Love** – love is synonymous with growth.[102] With a timeless perspective of oneness, see growth occurring. Be growth-

aware (or love-aware). Look through the lens of love and acquire a loving perspective.

Awareness – *Benefits*

- We become better **listeners**.
- We allow others to be **open in their communication**, creating trust – *the* foundation of an alliance.
- We become **connected** – with others, with the Universe and, ultimately, with our self.
- We acquire **vision**. We see the interconnectedness of disparate events unfold, and we see flow.
- We gain **confidence** as we realize the inevitability of new opportunities.

Be Lovingly Confrontational – shine your light with love and precision

We could describe this practice as a willingness and enthusiasm to "face the fire." Clearing up issues in any relationship brings insight and opportunity to the forefront. Problems no longer hold back the alliance. It is always better to deal with issues, and sooner is much better than later.

There are *always* good things on the other side of loving confrontation (when we co-face or co-front an issue *in* a relationship). Why wait?

Be Lovingly Confrontational – *Situation*

In alliances we are focused on *value*. However, there are many *hidden* and *unspoken issues* in any alliance which *impede* the ability to *find* and create value. Many of these issues themselves actually *contain* value. Value is hiding in our alliance. How do we find it?

First, we must examine the issues. Some issues are *seen* by everyone but dealt with by no one. These are the *unspoken issues* that afflict the entire alliance, the "elephant in the middle of the room."

People lack skills or motivation when it comes to being able to lovingly confronting that elephant. From a self-serving perspective they might calculate that it is not "politically expedient" to deal with such issues.[103] Or they are overcome by fear. This unspoken issue in the alliance could be low trust or unresolved cultural differences. It is possible that this elephant has been tolerated for years and now appears to be too large to be removed. We may have learned to "just walk around it and move on."

Then there are the *unseen issues*. These issues are hidden *in* an alliance's environment. This could be an issue, such as endemic fear and deep mistrust when working with a partner, especially a partner "everyone loves to hate."[104] There is so much fear that we cannot even talk about the topic of trust with this partner. There can be other problems we are not even aware of. We need to "dig up" the unseen and un-see-able issues in order to clear the path toward value.

There are two critically important issues which adversely affect any alliance's success: low trust and poor communications. What, if anything, can be done to *increase* trust? How can uncovering hidden and unaddressed issues improve trust and communications?

How can we uncover and deal with hidden issues in an alliance? Won't the uncovering of tough issues just "stir things up" and make things even worse?

Be Lovingly Confrontational – *Basic Ideas*

Life experience teaches us that the longer issues are kept hidden, the more fearful they become; problems *grow* in the dark.[105] With rare exception, facing an issue sooner is *always* better than avoiding it. Once we bring these things to light, once we look at them and take care of them, fear dissipates. We say, "That wasn't such a big deal. Why did I wait so long to deal with that issue?"

> *The hidden is kept apart, but value always lies in joint appreciation. What is concealed cannot be loved, and so it must be feared.*
>
> *- A Course in Miracles*

Some Spiritual Practices in Strategic Alliancing

Addicts and alcoholics in 12-step recovery programs experience tremendous relief after completing their 5th Step, after their "fearless and thorough moral inventory" is lovingly shared with a trusted other.[106] By bringing into the light one's honest self-assessment, fear's weightiness is gone and freedom from addiction is obtained. Through loving confrontation with a trusted other, integrity increases, and the disease of addiction is transformed into a blessing. A new spiritually-based life emerges, holding great insights and a new life (*newly found value*).

As alliance managers we are focused on *value*, so *joint appreciation* (i.e., loving confrontation) is a useful practice. First we need to differentiate between two very similar words:

- *Confrontation*: to *lovingly* "co-front" or *jointly face* an issue *between* – between two people or between two organizations. The motivation is *growth*. The focus is on what is going on *in* a relationship.

- *Conflict*: to *attack another* – another person or another organization. This is done to prove one is right and the other wrong. The motivation is to *judge* and place *blame*. The focus is on the other person or organization, not the issue in between.

The distinction between loving confrontation and conflict is subtle but *hugely* important. In the "heat of battle," during intense discussions, it is very easy to confuse confrontation with conflict. During such discussions we should continually ask ourselves:

- *Where* are we focusing our attention – **on the issue between**, or on *the other* (the other person or the other organization)?

- *How* are we focusing our attention – **in love** or in *judgment*?

- And the most important of all, what are our motives? *Why* are we confronting the issue - **to grow** or to *win*?

How we answer these questions actually depends upon whatever thought system we are relying on at that moment.[107] Are we spirit-based or love-based? Are we in love, knowing things will work out, with a sense of *connectedness*? Or are we in fear, focused on never-ending problems with a sense of *separateness*? Are we about *acceptance* or *judgment*?

Like other spiritual practices, confrontation starts within self. We first have to become aware of our chosen thought system. In addition, we grow by dealing with our internal integrity gaps and hypocrisies. Then we are better able to deal with hidden integrity gaps, or hidden issues, outside of ourselves. Through experience we know the healing growth that occurs with loving confrontation. We have learned this because we had to do this internal work with a trusted other (outside of recovery this is called "doing our work"). This experience gives us confidence and motivation. We know the value of confrontation. We know we need each other in order to draw closer to truth. We gain trust.

Alliances, whether internal (with self) or external (between companies), are *definitely* "we things." But we may *still* struggle to have loving confrontation without also having conflict.

How can we be "tough on issues and soft on people?"

It is helpful to use a metaphorical image.[108] Think of our attention as *light*. Light has amazing properties. First, by its mere presence, light eliminates darkness. As we shine our light on fear, it vanishes. Next, light has no sense of emotion; it has no shame, no blame and no judgment. Light is only interested in *seeing* things clearly.

Confrontation is also about seeing things clearly. It is about shining our shared lights *into* a relationship to look at issues and opportunities *in* that relationship. Shining our light on another person or on another company is conflict; this misuse of light can blind, disorient and upset others. So we need to be very careful *where* we are shining our light. Where and how are we focusing our attention? Where and how are we shining our shared light?

Some people might ask, is it helpful to simply shine our shared light on an issue, especially in business? Will managers accept this as a worthwhile thing to do? Besides, managers often tell us, "Bring me a solution, not a problem." But light itself can be the solution. In the physical world light disinfects objects.[109] In alliancing, our attention (light) neutralizes or enables *transcendence* over problems. As we shine our light on a situation, we come to understand it, we accept it, and we begin transcending it. It is no longer a problem. It is neutralized. We thoroughly examine a situation, and then we can accept it. Only then can we deal with it and rise above it.

The opportunity that is concealed within every problem does not manifest itself until all the facts of any given situation are openly acknowledged and fully accepted. This requires there to be no negative emotion (no fault-finding, no judgment and no blame) which creates defensiveness (more hiding).
As long as you deny that these problems exist, as long as you try to escape from them or wish that things were different, this window of opportunity will not open up,
and you remain stuck in that problematic situation, which will either stagnate or further deteriorate.

— Eckhart Tolle in *The Power of Now*
(paraphrased and parenthetic statements added)

The next stage after acceptance is *embracement*. Accepting a gift is one thing; embracing it, loving it or holding it near and dear is quite different. Love *is* growth. So, growing through a problematic situation is an act of love. Light, too, causes growth. As we continue to *lovingly shine our light* on a situation and embrace it, we *transform* it. At a minimum we learn insights hidden within the "problem." We learn more about the alliance and about each other. Such insights can be hugely valuable.

With time problems are further transformed into opportunity. In 12-step recovery, loving embracement of the disease of addiction occurs when we are of service to others. Such service, focused on the growth of another, is the embodiment of love. After a period of time, it is common to hear recovering addicts express deep gratitude for the spiritual awakening their disease has *given* them. Their disease was transformed into a blessing by oving embracement.

Acceptance transcends. Embracement transforms.

Spiritual Principles in Strategic Alliances

How is trust improved or created by confrontation?

Trust is *the* foundation of every relationship. Trust is the critical ingredient in open communications and effective negotiations. Trust and our ability to lovingly confront are critical in many of the spiritual practices discussed later. Both are necessary in the practices of *focusing collective attention, self-obsolescence, being an illuminating mirror* and *creating a productive community*. It is critically important to proactively *confront* lack of *trust* because trust is **the** foundation in every relationship and it is the basis for all spiritual practices.

It seems paradoxical to suggest that if trust is low, we should be confrontational in order to create more trust. If we are in an unhealthy alliance, with low trust, the tendency is to *avoid* confrontation for the sake of protecting the relationship. But confrontation actually "calls for" trust, so trust will come.

Think about how we develop personal attributes. We often put ourselves into situations requiring us to develop certain attributes. These situations "call for" those attributes, which come, and so we grow. We grow based on the situations we put ourselves into. For example, we may make bold moves in our career to further embolden ourselves. Such moves "call for" faith and trust, so we become more trustful and emboldened as a result of these situations. What is true for an individual is true for an organization. As we create a situation which "calls for" trust, trust will come. Most of us have experienced an interpersonal relationship that has become quite close and trust-filled as a result of a confrontation. We may have said, "After we 'cleared the air,' this 'enemy' of mine has become a dear friend."

This is not to say that we should artificially create problems or proactively seek out confrontational opportunities. But when we see a hidden issue and the need (or opportunity) for confrontation, we can actually be enthused. We realize that insight and opportunity lie hidden on the other side of any problem. From experience I know that, done in a loving manner, loving confrontation surfaces greatness.

The results of loving confrontation are *always* good. Goodness may come in the form of a deepening of that relationship or its termination. Either outcome is good. Either outcome is the best for both parties. In an alliance, "no deal," or the termination of an alliance, may be exactly the right thing; it *is* success.

Be Lovingly Confrontational – *Practical Steps*

1. Be *present* enough to be *aware* of what is going on *in* the alliance – between individuals and between the companies.
    a. Be aware of the *climate* in the alliance.
    b. See problems, successes and opportunities.
2. When problematic situations arise, address them as immediately and as directly as possible.
    a. Bring shared attention to bear; focus on the *issue*, not on each other.
    b. Fearlessly and thoroughly examine and accept the entire situation.
    c. Then embrace the situation, uncovering the solution and insights.
3. When *great* situations arise, address them, too, even more immediately than problems. Confrontation is not just for problems.
    a. Confront greatness – accept it, embrace it, and most importantly, share it.
    b. Experience the *power* in explicit, direct and sincere *gratitude*.
4. Discover and openly share with others the insights you gain in order to:
    a. Increasingly replicate greatness.
    b. Continually transcend and neutralize problems.
    c. Transform problems into insights and opportunity.
5. Over time, continually shine collective light on these situations.
    a. Healthy growth-oriented confrontation becomes part of

the alliance's DNA.
   b. Solve problems, gain insights, uncover opportunities … repeat and grow …

Be Lovingly Confrontational – *Spiritual Basis*

- **Love** – a realization that only goodness lies between us. There truly is nothing to fear, not even fear. In darkness problems grow, and they evaporate in the light of our collectively loving attention.

- **We Create** – our thoughts are light. Where and how we shine that light, collectively or individually, causes things to change and grow. Confrontation is an exercise in the transformational power of shared light. The first phase is *transcendence*, as we fully accept a situation. We neutralize the problem with our light. The next phase is *transformation*, as we lovingly embrace a situation. Problems become insight and opportunity. Goodness becomes greatness. Shine on!

- **Now** – there is no reason to wait. If not now, when? See problems and greatness; deal with them both – now. Problems get worse over time and the effect of gratitude diminishes over time.

Spirituality is not about sedate meekness and lowliness. It demands boldness and intensity:

> We can make our minds so like still water that beings gather about us, that they may see their own images, and so live for a moment with a clearer, perhaps even with a fiercer life because of our quiet.
>
> — William Butler Yeats

Be Lovingly Confrontational – *Benefits*

- **Issues** are more quickly uncovered and **dealt with**.
- **Successes** are quickly seen, acknowledged and **celebrated**.

- We enjoy more **open communication**.
- There is greater **trust** with others, both in the alliance and throughout the alliance.
- New **opportunities** are more easily **discovered**, leading to greater **value**-creation.

Be an Illuminating Mirror – see the good and reflect it back

This is a practice in authentically powerful gratitude. The best service we can give to another is to show them their own greatness, which they cannot see in themselves by themselves.

Be an Illuminating Mirror – *Situation*

Our job *is* about being of service. How can we be of maximal service to everyone around us?

Sometimes we struggle to maintain enthusiasm when motivation in the alliance wanes. What can we do in such situations?

Expressing gratitude is a great thing, but how can we do it in a way that is not contrived? How can we be *authentically* grateful? How can we express deeply felt appreciation?

It is so easy to get defocused by the negative, the drama and the complexity. How can we look past that stuff and stay focused on greatness and value?

Be an Illuminating Mirror – *Basic Ideas*

This exercise is explicitly about our most powerful and most loving use of light (our attention).

We are light. Thought is light. We need to continually be mindful of where and how we focus our attention, individually and collectively. Where and how is our light shining? That upon which light is shined grows.

Our best service to anyone is to be an "illuminating mirror."

We are at our best when we lovingly shine our light on, even into, another person. We help them see within themselves what they by themselves cannot see. We look past what they do or say, and we overlook their past. This is not to say that we avoid looking at what someone else does or says, or that we avoid looking at any of their past. We simply look *past* that superficial stuff.

We choose to focus our attention on *seeing the light in another* and reflecting that light back to them. This can apply to people and to companies. We consciously choose to see the *truth, light, love* and *greatness* within another. We see *the divine*, we see *the Infinite*, within. We then reflect that truth back so that they can see and accept this same truth, too. In love and through love we show the love within that we can see, but they cannot.

A huge byproduct of this practice is our increased awareness of our own truth, light, love and greatness. As we do to others, we do to ourselves. This practice is about our actions and our thoughts, most importantly our thoughts.

Finally, choose to see the collective greatness in the alliance and reflect that greatness back to all. Again, this is not to overlook the problems and challenges. It is to see those things, but then look past them. Deal with challenges and obstacles with practical recommendations, and then move on to accomplishing the alliance's greatest vision of value-creation.

Be an Illuminating Mirror – *Practical Steps*

1. As within, so without. Fearlessly go within yourself, with a trusted other, to see and embrace your own greatness. This is self-love. You cannot give away that which you do not know that you have.

2. Continually work to deepen the practices of *Presence* and *Awareness*. Be more fully present. Be more fully aware.

3. Continually work on *collective listening*. Hear the alliance speak of its greatness, especially its great potential for value; celebrate that greatness. Explicitly focus on individual and collective greatness.

4. Be deeply present and aware during one-on-one meetings or in group meetings. When you see the greatness within an individual or within the collective, do not be afraid to recognize greatness and acknowledge it. The recognition and acknowledgement parts of this work may occur at different times, and acknowledgement can be repeated many times.

5. Be specific and explicit. Be willing to boldly speak from your heart to other hearts. Tears of joyful, empathetic connection, especially in a fear-filled business context, are powerful and healthy things. They can be quite okay. Authentic gratitude is amazingly motivating for both the receiver and the giver.

6. Be sensitive to timing. You might gain awareness of greatness at one point in time and choose to acknowledge it at another point in time. You might see this greatness after the fact, during reflective meditative moments. Be patient. But when the opportunity does present itself, do not hesitate – that moment is the right time.

7. Be willing to accept compliments from others. It is better to focus on strengths, rather than on weaknesses. Accepting positive statements does not dull our competitive edge; it sharpens the inspirational side of that same sword. Stay present, look them in the eye, and acknowledge their love to you by saying, "Thank you." Accept this love in the grandeur of our collective "we-ness" – we cannot do this thing called life or alliancing alone.

8. Know that giving and receiving are one.

Be an Illuminating Mirror – *Spiritual Basis*

- **We Create** – our thoughts are light. Lovingly shine it onto and into others. See individual and collective greatness, and then reflect that light back.
- **We are Divine** – at our core is greatness.
- **Love** – at our core is greatness, nothing to fear. Love's purpose

is love. As we give love we get it back with gain. So, ultimately, all love is actually self love or selfish; more precisely, it is Self love or self-full love.[110]

- **Now** – stay mindful and present in the here and now.
- **Oneness** – the light I share with another I share with me. The love I show to another I show to me. Giving and receiving are one.

Be an Illuminating Mirror – *Benefits*

- A **healthier climate** in the alliance – more love and less fear – more abundance and less scarcity – more openness of communication and fewer secrets – greater trust.
- **Collaboration** and collaborative people are **attracted** to the alliance.
- Greater individual and collective **motivation.**
- Deepened **empathetic connectedness** – people feel more a part of, rather than apart from.

Consider two quotes from *A Course in Miracles*:

The truth in their minds reaches out to the truth in the minds of their brothers, so that illusions are not reinforced. They are thus brought to truth; truth is not brought to them.

The task of the miracle worker thus becomes to deny the denial of truth.[111] *The sick must heal themselves, for the truth is in them. Yet having obscured it, the light in another mind must shine into theirs because that light is theirs.*

Focus Collective Attention on Value – opportunities, problems, answers, ecosystem

By focusing collective attention on value, alliances are transformed.[112] To accomplish this we need to extend the application of *awareness, confrontation,* and *be an illuminating mirror,* so that the *transformational power of* **shared** *light* (this practice) can encompass an entire alliance. We need the collective light of our alliance focused on long-term *value creation*.

We can also use this practice to help solve our most vexing questions. And this simple 2-Slide Methodology™ can be used to help architect, develop and manage a business ecosystem.

The transcendental and transformational power of shared light is awesome.

Focus Collective Attention on Value – *Situation*

In a strategic alliance clear *organizational alignment* is crucial. With limited resources and strong independently-minded individuals with varied interests, our success as alliance managers hinges on our ability to achieve and maintain alignment. *Where* and *how* should the alliance be focused?

First of all, a chasm exists between companies. That chasm is comprised of cultural and strategic differences, the primary source of impediments to *value*-discovery and *value*-creation in any alliance. How can we help individuals span that chasm and work most effectively in the alliance?

We need to keep everyone focused on *value*: finding incremental *value* and removing *impediments* to that *value*. How do we do that?

Given the role an alliance plays in corporate strategy, we often participate in complex, strategically-impactful decisions. These decisions can affect the very existence of our own company and the health of an entire business ecosystem. A chosen course of action will often have unforeseen side effects. Can we use an alliance to help businesses find the best answer? And if so, how?

Focus Collective Attention on Value – *Basic Ideas*

This is an exercise of focusing collective attention. Again, it is helpful to think of our attention or our thoughts as *light*. Where our attention is focused, where our light is focused, grows. If we are looking for problems, we will find them. If we are looking for value-creating opportunities, we will find them. As the leader of an alliance, success depends on our ability to focus and continually refocus the alliance's collective light.

With their individual lights, individuals see bits and pieces of what is going on in an alliance. They see pieces of opportunity, pieces of problem and pieces of solution. If we as alliance managers want to *truly see* what is happening throughout our alliance, we need to *integrate* those pieces of light into a holistic picture. We need to be a value-enabling integrator. We integrate individual pieces into a collective whole so value-creating opportunities can be seen by all. This collective perspective sees unseen problems and unseen opportunity that individuals cannot see. We need others. We need others' perspectives.

Focusing collective attention relies upon the practice of loving confrontation. The clearer each individual's piece of a puzzle becomes, the better the integrated picture. Bold confrontation clarifies each piece and thereby improves the clarity of the overall view. And the result of confrontation is greater trust, which is critically important in this practice.

> *Two things are of paramount importance in any strategic alliance:*
> *(1) creating value, and*
> *(2) removing impediments standing in the way of the creation of that value.*

First – Creating Incremental Value. Many of these ideas are grounded in *The Program on Negotiation* and based on over 20 years of personal experience.[113] To uncover incremental value in any alliance, high trust and open communication are critical. We need to be able to creatively brainstorm in order to uncover the best teaming scenario. Each side needs to clearly understand the other side's fundamental business objectives (primary motives) and key underlying interests (surrounding motives) for collaborating. This requires great trust.

In a very real sense we are always negotiating in an alliance. We are constantly having substantive discussion. We are, therefore, always trying to understand each other better so we can find value and remove impediments. A rich collective understanding occurs as more individuals are heard. The hearing deepens in loving confrontational listening.[114] Our understanding stays fresh as we continually and deeply listen. This helps us uncover new value-creating opportunities, while also maintaining strong alignment throughout the alliance.

Figure 8.3a below shows an incremental value slide used in a $300 million deal between HP's printing business and SAP.[115] This slide was first developed in HP and then informally shared with two trusted others at SAP. SAP's initial reaction was, "No way! SAP does not do these kinds of deals!" Unbeknownst to HP this slide then "took on a life of its own," and it resurfaced two months later as part of some newly emerging corporate-level HP/SAP discussions.[116] Three months after that, the rest of the broader HP-wide initiative unraveled, and our deal, as captured in this slide, became the only initiative between HP and SAP. Nine months later, we closed on our contractual negotiations with SAP. This alliance was then publicly announced at SAP's SAPPHIRE event a year later.

So, to recap, over a three-year period, this one simple slide took HP from "no way" to "a given" to "the only initiative left standing" to a signed contract and then to a joint HP/SAP announcement.[117] Such is the power of focusing collective attention. Such is the power of simplicity.

During this time we continually reviewed, revised and used this slide as a living document. We were always listening deeply to anyone and everyone in the alliance; we heard their valuable ideas and continually refined the slide. We used it as a catalyst to stir up and deepen communication in meetings and in one-on-one discussions.

This slide helped the alliance stay aligned and focused. It helped us maintain focus during often tumultuous contract negotiations. It gave us something to refer back to when briefing executives, developing marketing plans, creating sales tools or briefing industry analysts.

This slide established our alliance's value-creating vision.

Spiritual Principles in Strategic Alliances

SAP/HP – strategic business context SAP/NetWeaver / HPDS – 12 Nov 2003; Walldorf, DE (R. Wedel, C. Wachter, A. Cooke and J. Kittel)	
Fundamental Business Objectives	
SAP's	HP's
• Spring '04 public **endorsement of SAP Web AS** • significantly reduce **TCO** & increase customer satisfaction – new SAP strategic imperative • remove "(printing &) output" **pain** for SAP & SAP's customers • influence license **sales** – up-/cross-selling to installed base & sales to new customers • help SAP reduce investments – **focus on core** business objectives vs. spooling	• **broad deployment** of HP OMS solutions • deliver on "**printing in the enterprise**" Corp Obj • increase license & services **sales** for HP's OMS solutions (HPOS & HPDS) • leverage off all of **HP's enterprise strengths** – output management, systems management, enterprise systems & services • raise "output" considerations **earlier** w/customers
Key Underlying Interests	
SAP's	HP's
• accelerate adoption of **Adobe forms**, return on SAP investments • reduce SAP customer **support**, re: output	• **differentiate** HP on-/off-ramp devices • accelerate growth in "printing in the enterprise" services
Possible Teaming Scenarios • engineering-level relationship to port **HPDS to Web AS 6.30/6.40** • TCO-driven, **tightly-integrated HPDS/WAS packaged solutions** (e.g., CRM, Fin, Sales & Dist'n – maybe w/ DP&P or DPS for more strategic solution) – e.g., unified install, mgmt, etc. • **OEM core output management module** in NetWeaver (tee-up in exec-level briefing – vision) • **SAP/Adobe/HP forms+output triad solutions** • explore **mid-market/SMB** plays	

Figure 8.3a – Focus collective attention on incremental value.

Second – Removing Value-Impediments. These ideas are also derived from *The Program on Negotiation*, over 20 years of personal experience, plus consulting with Vantage Partners LLC.[118]

The greatest obstacle impeding value-creation in an alliance is the chasm between the partners. This chasm is comprised of differences in corporate culture and divergent strategies. Assessing a company's culture and strategy can be overwhelmingly complex and daunting. In an alliance this gets simplified when we focus on *working* together and when we listen to the people who are actually *doing* that work.

When things are not working in an alliance, we often hear such statements as, "I cannot trust him; he is devious," or "He does not know what he is doing; he is an idiot."[119]

When we interpret the behavior of another as a sign of deviousness or incompetency, that misinterpretation is a sign. It

Some Spiritual Practices in Strategic Alliancing

is a sign of unacknowledged differences in perspective.

When others see themselves and the world differently than we do, they behave differently than we expect. The solution is not to label and judge their behavior. The answer is to understand their perspective, to see things as they see them. In an alliance each company's *perspective* is determined by their respective corporate cultural, strategy and other divisive issues.[120]

If both companies understand the other company's perspective, they will naturally understand the cultural and strategic differences. With this understanding the behavior of the other side becomes more rational. Then each side will naturally understand how to bridge the cultural and strategic chasm and will authentically know how to work more effectively together.

This sharing of perspective is similar to the incremental value work discussed earlier. It is done by deeply or *confrontationally listening* to as many people as possible who work in the alliance. We listen to both sides of the alliance. We focus on two simple questions, asked in different ways:

- **Top-of-mind**, when you *think* about **the other company**, what do you *think*? When you *look* at the other, what do you *see*?

- **Top-of-mind** – when you *think* about **your own company**, what do you *think*? When you *look* at your own company, what do you *see*?

The focus is on our *working relationship*. We are interested in hearing about issues that affect the ability to *collaborate*. We are not interested in anything else. By openly, boldly and unemotionally sharing our perspective *across* the chasm that divides us, we end up *seeing* the chasm more clearly.

As we hear the voice of the collective we ask people to be as clear, bold and direct as possible. We need to hear about the most troublesome problems they see or experience in the alliance. We need to hear of their biggest issues and the hidden issues (the "elephant in the room"). For some topics it will be important to emphasize that personal anonymity is naturally preserved as we listen and then integrate individual issues into the collective voice; we can honestly say, "I don't know who said that," when challenged to identify the individual source of a statement. This exercise is about seeking the truth, not exposing individuals.

In 1997, we established HP's corporate-level strategic alliance with Microsoft. During the first few years, academics, consultants and our own experience told us, "No two high-technology companies' cultures differed more radically than Hewlett-Packard's and Microsoft's."[121] We desperately needed some way to help people quickly "get it" – to help us work better together.

From 1997 to 2002, we developed and continually refined one simple slide that helped hundreds of HP/Microsoft alliancing teams "get it." Figure 8.3b is that slide.[122] It is clear, bold and direct. Some of the points addressed emotionally-charged issues as unemotionally as possible. It is better that an issue gets raised, even in an emotionally-charged manner, than to not get raised at all. This one slide conveyed collective reality as seen by those *working* in the alliance. It helped people see the other's perspective. With specific recommendations it then helped people span across the differences. It increased the effectiveness of the alliance.

In 2000, this one slide was used to get a $20 million hosted Exchange deal back "on track."[123] The HP and Microsoft sales teams were trying to collaboratively sell this solution to American Express in Phoenix, Arizona. Within one hour, I got two separate phone calls – one from the HP sales lead, and one from his counterpart. Each was labeling the other as devious *and* incompetent. They both wanted the other taken off the account. After discussing the slide in detail with each separately and then collectively, tensions softened. Both sides saw the other in a different light. They were able to work more collaboratively. They "got it."

Some Spiritual Practices in Strategic Alliancing

 *Microsoft*

HP/MS Cultural Differences (1997-2002, Nov 2007 HBR article)

Cultural Differences	
HP's View of Microsoft	**Microsoft's View of HP**
• Excessively competitive and confrontational • Controlling, paranoid and greedy (MS's unstated values) • "Win / don't care" partnering mindset • Focused only on the deal • Packaged software mentality – commoditizes everything, including partnering	• A non-player in professional services • Falling behind its competitors • Slow, bureaucratic – a laggard • Unable to execute consistently and predictably • Conflicted sales strategies in the field (UNIX vs. NT in late '90s)
HP's View of HP	**Microsoft's View of Microsoft**
• Collaborative partnering mind-set – looks for the common good • Reinventing – trying to get more focused under new CEO's leadership (Fiorina) • Disciplined – takes a long-term, mature approach to evaluation market opportunities • Win/win partnering – actively seeks the other company's wins • Flexible – looks for creative deals	• Competitive, fast-moving and entrepreneurial • "Our products are changing the world in profoundly positive ways" • Center of the new economy • Focuses on objectives and assumes others do the same • Misunderstood: the world doesn't realize what positive things the company does for everyone • Brings partners into deals, expecting they will be grateful and go get the business without continued hand-holding
Recommendations	
• Focus on complementary strengths – HP's: complex sol'n selling, long-term relations & perspective, risk-mitigating, collaborative; MS's: product expertise, short-term wins, rapid decision-making, risk-taking, competitive orientation. • Align to different perspectives – MS is focused on competitive wins, HP is focused on delivering value to customers. • For HP: align into MS's perspective, assertively sell HP's strengths, under set & over-deliver on expectations.	

Figure 8.3b – Focus collectively on value-impediments, especially recommendations (the solution).

That which light (our attention) shines on grows. The purpose of this slide is not to focus on *problems*, but to focus on *solutions* – practical recommendations. First, we *do* need to fully acknowledge and accept the problems, only then can we *look past* the problems toward the solutions.

In terms of both of these slides – incremental value and value-impediments – we continually listen deeply and collectively. We then coalesce what we hear (oneness) and we share it back to achieve alignment. We iteratively listen, coalesce input, refocus attention, and listen again. These two slides are living documents; they constantly evolve through this reiterative process.

As alliance managers we are leaders in focusing collective attention. Shared light has the power to *transcend* problems and *transform* them into opportunity – this is an exercise in true growth – this is an exercise in love.

As we establish and maintain focus and alignment in an alliance, the results are stunning.

Third – Confronting Difficult Decisions. We can also use the practice of focusing collective attention as a tool to help our company make better decisions. When faced with complex challenges, companies tend to rely on upper management, outside consultants, or corporate business planners to recommend strategic options. To augment management's work we can also "ask an alliance." An alliance *will* see details and side effects that others *will* often miss.

In large alliances, often at the center of an ecosystem, alliance managers already wrestle with complex issues with far-reaching impact.[124] Why not *use* those alliances who are already involved in the very issues the company is wrestling with? Ask the people on the front line of these issues. Collectively listen to that alliance and carry its message back into the corporation to improve strategic planning.[125]

Today's strategic challenges are too broad and complex for decisions to be made by a select few. Broad collaborative decision-making is what is needed.

Fourth – Ecosystem Management. By focusing collective attention on value we are able to describe the essence of an alliance in two simple slides: (a) incremental value and (b) value-impediments. This *simplicity* allows us to have a commonly-agreed-upon tool with our partner. Simplicity also provides a means for managing a set of alliances in a layer in our business ecosystem. After we have developed enough of the two slide sets to represent an ecosystem layer, we can start applying this practice in the ecosystem. The alliance-specific slides are creatively coalesced into two slides that represent common types of alliance partners. These two "abstracted up" slides represent our company's collective view of the value and challenges we see *in* part of the ecosystem.[126]

Figure 8.3c illustrates two simple slides that represent a layer of the ecosystem. Insights from these slides can drive ecosystem management processes for our company. We develop programs focused on (a) common value-creation/-extraction activities or (b) the removal of value-impeding obstacles in that layer. After developing two slides for other layers of the ecosystem, we see more clearly how value gets progressively created and extracted from layer-to-layer. We develop ecosystem management programs which (a) drive that value-creation process through the layers toward our customers. We develop programs to (b) neutralize value-impediments within each layer and across the ecosystem. Such is the practical power in *simplicity*.

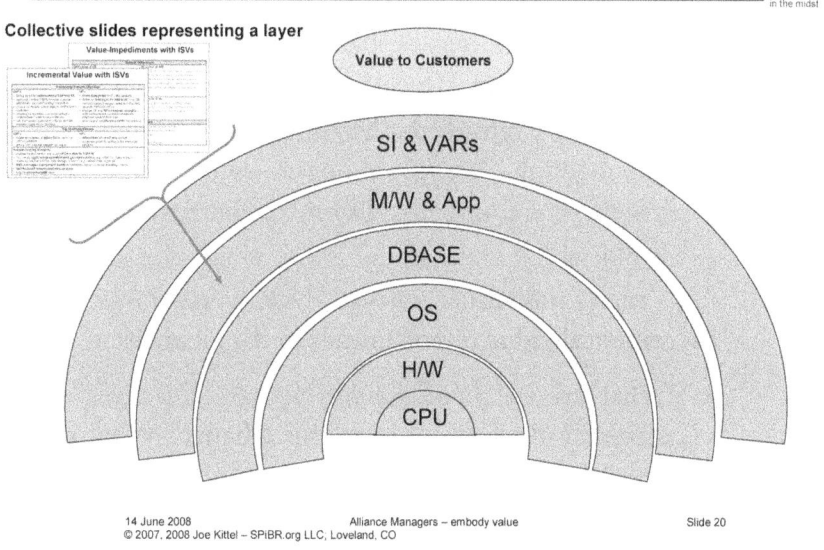

Figure 8.3c – Ecosystem layer-specific focus on value and impediments.

Focus Collective Attention on Value – *Practical Steps*

1. Listen deeply to everyone working in the alliance. Ask probing, thought-provoking questions.

2. Listen to people from every layer of the organization – from the front-line "worker bee" to the top-most executive.

3. Listen to people from every functional area involved – from R&D-to-Sales, Legal, Finance, HR, etc.

a. Start with a series of one-on-one meetings.
b. Bring collective listening and sharing activities into meetings.
c. Coalesce what you hear. What is the alliance holistically saying?
   i. What does the alliance see as its opportunities and vision for the future?
   ii. What are the challenges? What are solutions to those challenges?
   iii. Opportunities, problems and answers all reside *in* the alliance. Hear it?
d. Over time, refresh the listening with in-depth one-on-one meetings. Vary from one-on-one to group settings. Listen, share, align, re-listen, re-share, re-align, re-re-listen …

4. Ask each individual about their perspective on the **incremental value** opportunities in the alliance:
   a. What are the *fundamental business objectives* for this alliance? Why do we have this alliance? What do they see as the primary reasons we are working together?
   b. Are there missed business opportunities? Are there new value-creating ideas?
   c. What are the *key underlying interests* for this alliance? Given we will achieve success in the fundamental business objectives, what will be side benefits we can derive from this alliance?
   d. Focus on looking for and pointing out to others both *intangible* forms of value and *long*-term forms of value. Use this exercise to continually expand the notion of value beyond near-term tangible forms.[127]

5. Ask each individual about their perspective on the **value-impediments** standing in the way of creating incremental value.

Some Spiritual Practices in Strategic Alliancing

   a. As we work together, what are our biggest challenges?
   b. When you look at or think about the other side, *what comes to mind*?
   c. As you look at or think about your own company, *what comes to mind*?
   d. What are the toughest issues that everyone avoids talking about? What are the "elephants in the middle of the room" that people avoid, hoping they will go away?
6. Continually take individual inputs and coalesce them into a collective picture of incremental value and value-impediments. Simplify – simplify – simplify. Strive to have no more than five points in each cell of the table – distill down without losing key points. Strive to be bold, clear and maybe a bit contentious.
7. Stir things up. Get people to think deeply about this stuff.
8. Obsess on these two slides. Always have them with you. Always refer to them. Always look for ways to improve the slides based on ongoing activities, meetings, conference calls and in-depth one-on-one discussions. Continually look for opportunities to share these insights with others and gather their inputs into the slides.
9. See these two simple slides evolve to embody the long-term vision for the alliance and the basis for near-term tactical planning.
10. Listen … coalesce … share … refocus … listen …
11. Use this methodology to help the company make better strategic decisions.
12. After listening to enough alliances, start listening to the ecosystem.

Focus Collective Attention on Value – *Spiritual Basis*

- **Oneness** – we hear what the alliance is collectively saying by deeply listening to as many people as possible throughout the alliance. This is an ongoing process – continually listen.

- **We create** – this is an exercise of getting *collective attention focused*, and then continually refocused, on the critical essence in an alliance – incremental value and value-impediments. Where and how we focus collective attention grows.

- **Love** – it is always a good thing to deeply explore difficult issues in any relationship. There is nothing to fear. Fear comes from keeping things hidden. Goodness comes when these things are exposed to light.

Focus Collective Attention on Value – *Benefits*

- **True leadership** of the alliance. We lead by showing others where collective thought should be focused: (a) incremental value and (b) value-impediments. Looking elsewhere is a distraction.

- **Insights** from the alliance. Insights into the alliance. The answers, problems and answers to problems lie in relationships. Look there. Listen there.

- **Increased effectiveness** via greater focus in the alliance. Focus on value and practical recommendations for overcoming impediments. We learn how to work better together.

- **Greater success.** Individually and collectively.

- With just two slides you will **always be able to answer the questions:** How is the alliance going? What are the problems? And (we love to hear this question) How can I help?

- By referring to these two slides we will be able to **add value in any discussion** with anyone, anywhere, any time.

- These two slides can be the **jointly-agreed-to core work between the partners**, and across all partners of similar type in an area of the business ecosystem. They simply and succinctly talk about value and how to get to more. What else is there?

- Through simplicity, the **groundwork** is laid for **ecosystem management**.

Negotiate – open, trust-filled and focused; just-enough, just-in-time preparation

Negotiating *is* a spiritual practice. It is a practice of open, trust-filled discussions aimed at finding the best solution for all. Simplicity is a powerful tool in negotiating; it can keep us focused on value. Formal negotiations can be a time to train our alliance team and give them just-in-time and just-enough training in relationship-building concepts and the nuances of alliancing.

Negotiate – *Situation*

As strategic alliance managers we are *always* negotiating. We are always engaged in substantive discussions which impact our company – this *is* negotiating.

If we are always negotiating, does that mean we are always preparing? If so, how do we prepare?

How can we make sure the best value-creating results are achieved – for our company and the other company, near-term and long-term?

How can we not be taken advantage of by an aggressive "cut-throat" negotiator?

Negotiate – *Basic Ideas*

Negotiating *is* a pervasively critical alliancing skill. It is helpful to take formal negotiating training.[128] These skills are not just for special "negotiating" events; they are critical throughout our day. We *are* always negotiating.

In its most effective form negotiating *is* spiritual.[129] Both *The Program on Negotiation* and the book *Getting to Yes* describe the following nontraditional negotiating concepts grounded in spiritual principles:

- Achieve a **collective state of abundance** – grounded in *oneness*, *love* and *we are divine*.

- **Focus on** the **problem** and issues *between* people, not with the people – grounded in *love, we create, now*, the practice of *being lovingly confrontational* and the concept that spirit lives *in* a relationship.

- **Openly explore options** – grounded in *we are divine, we create* and the critical need for *trust*.

Trust is fundamental in effective negotiating. Trust is created and sustained via spirituality (*oneness, we are divine*, and *being lovingly confrontational*).

In an alliance, negotiating is about creating abundant *value* and achieving collective *greatness*.

A clear understanding of both companies' (a) incremental *value* and (b) value-*impediments* forms the basis for negotiations.[130] These two simple slides are helpful in both informal day-to-day negotiations and formal negotiations. With the establishment of this foundation we creatively brainstorm with the partner on the best value-creating and impediment-removing teaming scenarios – that *is* negotiating. These two slides help us to avoid getting distracted by complexity and drama; we stay focused on our core issues.

The remainder of this section is *not* intended to replace formal negotiation training, but to highlight key preparatory activities for alliance managers, done prior to formal negotiating events.

We first negotiate with our own management. With them we define the core team, people who will directly participate in the negotiations. *Before* negotiating, define the **N, L** and **I** roles:

- Those with whom we must **Negotiate**; people with whom the outcome of the negotiation must align.

- Those to whom we must **Listen**; hear them out at the beginning, although they may disagree with the outcome.

- Those whom we need to **Inform** at various steps along the way.

Finally, what is the timing for major **N, L** and **I** activities?

Some Spiritual Practices in Strategic Alliancing

Come to an understanding ahead of time about the critical terms and conditions that *must* be addressed during negotiation. Then check these issues against the (a) incremental value and (b) value-impediments slides previously developed. Are these critical issues covered by these two slides, or was something missed during the slides' development? What internal reconciliation is needed before negotiating with the other side?

Think ahead of time. Think about both companies' BATNAs (**b**est **a**lternative **t**o **n**o **a**greement), possible teaming scenarios, and standards of legitimacy (ideas that will help get negotiations unstuck, moving both sides toward favorable outcomes).[131]

Prior to each substantive interaction with the other side, determine ahead of time how information will be managed. What information will be shared, learned and kept?

Timing is an all-important area for preparation. Understand key time-based stake-in-the-ground milestones. How will time affect the negotiations from both side's perspectives? How can you increase patience on your side so that time cannot be used against your own company?

It is important to prepare the core team on the right issues at the right time. As alliance managers we lead others as to where collective thought needs to be focused. In order to proactively drive discussions, our core team should be thinking a bit more deeply and a bit further out in time than the other side – just a bit. We practice just-enough and just-in-time preparation.

Living by spiritual principles gives us clarity, boldness and confidence. These principles are *especially* helpful in negotiations. The other side may be playing by different rules or operating in a different thought system – that is okay.[132] One enlightened side, one enlightened person, can be enough. We will change the outcome of the negotiations by our embodiment of simple truths.[133]

Spiritual Principles in Strategic Alliances

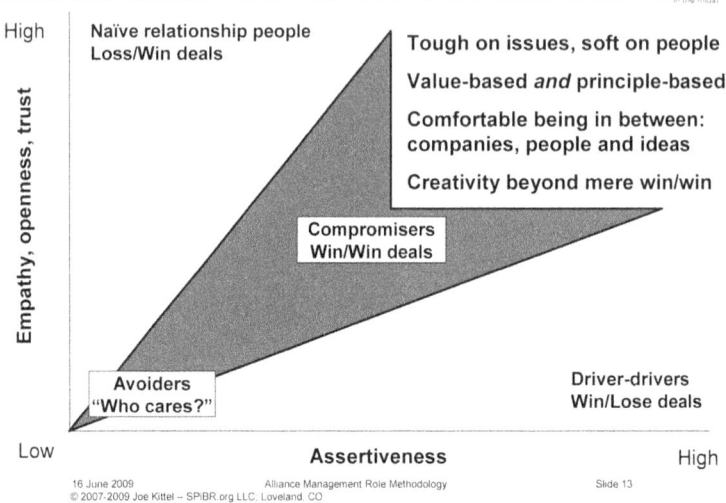

Figure 8.5 – The Best Negotiators: tough on issues, soft on people, comfortable in between.

Figure 8.5 illustrates the creative spirit that lives *between* two *ideas*. When we can keep collective attention focused on the tension between the ideas of *empathy* and *drive*, we achieve results beyond simplistic compromise. The best example of this is seen during creative brainstorming when we are wrestling between option A and option B. We push, but we push hard with empathy. We are intense and loving. We keep attention focused on issues, not people or companies. The process of creative brainstorming takes collective attention back and forth across *the space between* options A and B. Suddenly someone says "How about option C?" which is not a simplistic compromise between A and B, but a fundamentally new third option, beyond compromise and beyond win/win. The true test of solution C is whether or not it is "the right thing for all concerned," for both companies, for the ecosystem and even for competitors.

Negotiate – *Practical Steps*

1. Prepare around attitude &mindset; orient collective thought

Some Spiritual Practices in Strategic Alliancing

toward abundance. Focus on creating or expanding a pie versus dividing a pie.

2. Prepare self and others – he who prepares best "wins." Winning may not seem to be especially spiritual. But if you are focused on the right thing for all, it is "right" to lead the negotiating process. Prepare *before* formal negotiations commence.

3. Prepare for *any* substantive discussion. During contractual negotiations prepare *just enough* and *just in time* for each discussion, do not overload the team with too much detail too fast. Prepare for any meaningful discussion outside of formal contractual negotiations.

4. Use the two slides of (a) incremental value and (b) value-impediments as the centerpiece for preparation and negotiations. There is great power in simplicity. These two slides capture what is collectively being sought out and what stands in the way of that goal. The negotiating process will likely affect the content of these two slides – that is okay.

5. Define the decision-making process *before* you enter into formal negotiations. With the executive sponsor define the core team, extended team and the **N, L** and **I** roles. When a negotiation becomes intense, some individuals may try to impose their will on the negotiations. During these times refer back to the previously agreed-to roles to maintain organizational alignment.

6. Put yourself in the other's shoes/head. Think about both company's respective BATNAs and creative teaming scenarios. Be prepared to "kick start" the negotiations for the other side if it is hard for them to substantively and positively engage.

7. Prepare standards of legitimacy – legitimate reference points to refer to in order to get negotiations unstuck.

8. Prepare on the topic of *time*. How might time be used by

either side? How can you defuse time's adverse effect on your company? How can you give others and management greater patience? Remind others of the inevitability of the value-creating vision for the alliance.

Negotiate – *Spiritual Basis*

- **Love** – the most effective negotiating, in a long-term value-creating alliance, is not "hard-nosed" negotiating. The best outcomes are achieved with a sense of abundance, which is love-based. Fear-based environments produce a scarcity mindset of "me vs. you," where we are dividing up a fixed resource. The best long-term negotiating environment is high in trust and empathetic rapport building, leading to deep interpersonal relationships. Love is assertive; it is focused on growth. Love demands the right outcome for all concerned. In such a setting jointly-explored teaming scenarios are openly discussed. The most difficult issues are addressed without negative emotion. The best negotiating is grounded in love.[134]

- **We create** – the negotiating process is an exercise in collective thoughtfulness – thought creates. It is critical that collective attention stays focused on the right things, at the right time, and in the right manner.

- **We are Divine** and **Oneness** – respect and rapport is high. We realize, via oneness, that the best answers lies between us. Spirit lives *in* a relationship. Great negotiating is a "we thing."

Negotiate – *Benefits*

- Better outcomes. Greater **value-creation**. Deals that stand the test of time.

- Negotiating processes that *improve* and *deepen* relationships – interpersonally and between the companies.

Self-Obsolescence – giving and receiving are one; always *be* value

This practice is definitely nontraditional. It is alien to how most people behave in business. It is about empowering and emboldening others so that we can become empowered and emboldened. It is ultimately about the realization that *giving* and *receiving* are *one*. It is living or *being* the Golden Rule. What we give, we get back; so give, give value, and we will become the *embodiment* of value.

Self-Obsolescence – *Situation*

This section is about a spiritual practice that is comprehensive in nature. In order to introduce the ideas in this section we ask a comprehensive question – as alliance managers, what are we to do? Given that:

- most alliances *fail*, due to *poor relationships* – intercompany and interpersonal relationships;
- in an increasingly-interconnected, globally-distributed value chain, *alliances are increasingly important;*
- our job is about "*doing the impossible with nothing*" – with insufficient resources in our direct control, we are about getting highly-competitive companies to collaborate.

How can we increase our ability to influence the alliance? We lack sufficient power and our ability to influence is limited. We cannot be everywhere and in the middle of every activity. How can we increase the depth and breadth of our influence?

Self-Obsolescence – *Basic Ideas*

We need to boldly employ *nontraditional* tactics, *alien* in traditional business, in order to:

- improve and *deepen relationships*, and
- create *greater incremental value*.

We need a *nontraditional* and *alien* change in attitude & mindset, toward ourselves and about our role in business.

The comprehensive answer to this complex situation is shockingly simple.

We should strive to obsolete ourselves.

The reasonable question you might ask is, "Are you nuts?!" In today's business climate, a conscious attempt at self-obsolescence is seen by many as reckless at best and career suicide at worse. Why should we even consider self-obsolescence? Bear with us, read on, and see if this idea rings true for you. See if there are some simple, nontraditional and uniquely helpful ideas in this section.

This spiritual practice is the core of a fundamentally healthy change in our attitude & mindset – toward others, toward self and toward the alliance. This practice will change the climate in the alliance, improve communications and create trust.

The "basic idea" here *is* **ideas**.

The idea being that when ideas are shared or extended, they grow and they return back to us with gain. When we give of ideas, we receive back. When we give of ourselves, we receive back – we gain and we grow – collectively and individually.

> *Complete possession is proved only by giving.*
> *All you are unable to give possesses you.*
>
> \- André Gide – French author and
> 1947 winner of Nobel prize in literature

Our business colleagues rightfully expect us to be the most all-knowing source of information about our alliance. We are expected to be able to answer, "How is it going? What is this alliance all about? What are the issues? How can we best work together?" We should be able to answer these questions, posed by anyone, at any time, and anywhere. The 2-Slide Methodology™ discussed in the section titled *Focus Collective Attention on Value* will provide us with the answers to all of these questions. We gain insights as we listen holistically to, and then share back, with the alliance:

Some Spiritual Practices in Strategic Alliancing

- opportunities to *create incremental value* – what the alliance is about;
- *value-impediments* – the greatest challenges with *practical recommendations*.

Over time the two slides which summarize these ideas become increasingly valuable. Their value grows as they are shared. We continually look for new insights to improve the ideas.

Our ideas *are* our greatest possessions. What are we without our ideas? Some spiritual thinkers go so far as to say that man is simply *an idea in the mind of the Infinite*. So perhaps *we* are an idea. This idea is deep; think about it. This ends up changing the very notion of what it means to give of one's Self. When we are giving, we are actually giving an idea from one idea (you) to another idea (another). And when an idea is given away, we don't lose it; in fact, ideas (in this case all three of them) are strengthen by the act of giving.

A traditional philosophy in business is, "knowledge is power"; therefore, we should hoard our ideas. But if, as alliance managers, we hoard our ideas, we will stifle the alliance, and we will fail. We *must* share and extend our best ideas to others. We must extend into the alliance, or give away, critically important ideas:

- Organizational, strategic, cultural and technical **details about the partner** – help each other understand the other side – help each other engage with the other side as effectively as possible.

- Practical recommendations for **bridging the cultural and strategic chasms** between the companies (value-impediments).

- An **expanded notion of value** – willingness to value intangible forms of value; patience when considering longer-term forms of value; and valuing *relationship* as a business asset.

- An **expanded notion of time** – the strategic importance of presence and patience in alliancing.

- Share via **just-in-time and just-enough training** – alliance-specific skills and knowledge such as listening; rapport building; trust building; negotiation; use of informal teaming documents, critical legal and regulatory issues, ecosystem and competitive issues; communication; performance metrics; expectation-setting; escalation and confrontation.

- Through **personal embodiment**, *be* a practical example of relationship-deepening spiritual ideas, such as *oneness*, *now*, *our divine nature* and *creative ability*, and *love*.[135]

The overall idea is to strive to "obsolete" ourselves. Consciously strive to enable others so they no longer *need* us. Teach others our best ideas in a manner appropriate for the audience and setting.[136] We then experience less *neediness* and a greater *wanting* of us by others. We experience a giving back from others. They give back their ideas to us as we freely give ours to them – this reciprocal giving back is a natural human tendency.[137] Others will naturally include us in their activities; we won't have to force them to give us updates. We will attract collaboration. Our influence will pervade the alliance. We will grow in our virtual presence throughout the alliance as our informal power increases. We are empowered as we empower, which allows us greater empowerment – *we* become a virtuous cycle. We become "the eye of the hurricane."

This is how we *increase* our personal *power* and *influence*, by giving of ourselves, by freely giving our ideas to others, by striving to obsolete ourselves. Power and influence increase as we extend ourselves, as we extend our ideas to others.

We *are* about the obsolescence of our *little* self – our sense of self based on ego, fear, separation and scarcity. In return we rediscover our greater Self – self which is based on spirit, love, connectedness and abundance. Done rightly, our job is "*all* about us and *nothing* about us" – both at the same time. We are about being self-full so others can be self-full, too. Collective grandeur is our aim.

Our job is about grandeur, rather than grandiosity. Alliancing is not about any one individual's singular grandiosity – there is no place for egomaniacs in an alliance – they will destroy an alliance. Alliancing *is* about our individual *and* collective grandeur – *both* are achieved together – they are inexorably linked.

Self-Obsolescence – *Practical Steps*

1. Prerequisites for the practice of *Self-Obsolescence* are included in prior sections in this chapter – *Presence, Awareness, Being Lovingly Confrontational*, and *Focusing Collective Attention on Value*. That work provides us with the *valuable* content we will now *extend* into our alliance. We will then *embody* value.

2. Think of the needs of others in the alliance. What do they need in order to be successful? Provide others with the following:

   a. Clear articulation of **all forms of value** potentially created in this alliance – with special emphasis on intangible and long-term forms.

   b. A clear, crisp long-term **vision** – use it to promote patience, persistence and tenacity.

   c. An overview of each company's **decision-making processes**, including organizational details – describe how resources get committed.

   d. Summaries of key **strategic**, technical, regulatory and ecosystem **issues**.

   e. Focused recommendations for **engagement effectiveness**, how individuals can overcome value-impediments.

   f. Just-enough and **just-in-time training**, based on *the* next step in the alliance, especially: negotiating, listening, trust building, open communication and confrontation.

3. Share your greatest ideas, wisdom and insights with anyone, everyone and always. Be of value, embody value, be value. Be aware of and mindful of the audience. Share your ideas that will most empower others; make it so they do not *need* you. Obviously, great care must be taken with confidential information and intellectual property rights; but most of an alliance manager's most precious personal value (our ideas) falls outside of these restricted areas.

4. Be prepared to accept and embrace the reciprocal giving back from others of their ideas, insights and alliancing activities. When they naturally are attracted toward you in the spirit of inclusion, acknowledge it with *gratitude* toward them and toward your Self.

5. As your power, presence and ideas grow, *stay humble*. Accept this growth with a sense of grandeur by remaining "part of" – alliancing is "a we thing." You could not have done this without *them*.

6. As your insights grow, be bold. You will *gain insights* that others *cannot see*. Boldly share these insights with others, especially management. At times this will seem like a lonely task, as you share both success-filled and unpleasant ideas. Others won't readily see what you see. Your job is to patiently and persistently *paint the picture* so others can see what you see.

7. Fasten your seat belt. Be prepared for individual and collective greatness.[138]

Self-Obsolescence – *Spiritual Basis*

- **Oneness** – given the oneness of us all, when I give of myself to another I am really giving *to* my Self. Giving and receiving are one.

- **Love** – goodness and growth prevail. This practice is about sharing for the sake of growth. It is about love. This practice assumes love, it calls for love and love comes. It is all about love.

- **We Create** – creation occurs through the sharing of ideas. The more good ideas are freely shared, the better. Creation is accomplished in the extending of ideas.

Self-Obsolescence – *Benefits*

- An **increase** in personal **power, presence** and **effectiveness**.
    - More **fun** than one person deserves!

- A more effective **value-creating alliance**.

Every good teacher hopes to give his students so much of his own learning that they will one day no longer need him. Thoughts increase by being given away. The more we believe in them the stronger they become. Everything is an idea. How, then, can giving and losing be associated?[139]

— A Course in Miracles

Ours is actually a "service job." We are about being of maximal helpful service to others in the alliance, everyone, everywhere, all the time. We are *of* value in order to *create* value.

Transforming an Alliance into a Productive Community – an attractive home

This practice is actually a vision for our alliance's possibility. The possibility is to transform an alliance into a productive community.

Transforming an Alliance into a Productive Community – *Situation*

Today's business structures are hierarchical. Their mode of operation is one of *telling* people what to do with resultant power struggles and political gamesmanship. In this climate we, alliance managers, are expected to establish a collaborative value-producing alliance. These nontraditional business relationships have to exist within the highly-competitive, fear-dominated world of business. But an alliance is most effective if it has a collaborative-oriented climate.[140]

In the earlier section titled *Focus Collective Attention on Value*, we started developing a value-creating vision for our alliance. This vision describes the *substance* of an alliance, the value it creates. Can we also develop a vision for the *form* of a strategic alliance? Perhaps substance and form *have to* evolve in parallel. Perhaps substance and form are the cause and effect of each other. Is there a virtuous cycle where growth in *substance* changes *form* and the new form enables greater *value*?

Perhaps there is another way to think about an alliance's structure. Maybe there is a *nontraditional* model for an alliance that is more aligned with its purpose to *create* value. How can such a model exist within the traditional hierarchy of business?

Transforming an Alliance into a Productive Community – *Basic Ideas*

As we collectively see and holistically share the core vision we see for our alliance, and as the alliance progresses toward its value-creating vision, the informal *form* of our alliance will evolve. As an alliance's form evolves, its ability to create value increases. Growth affects both form and substance, leading to a more growth-oriented alliance. The alliance becomes a productive community with a clearer sense of purpose.

This sense of community starts within Self, spreads to a few trusted others, and extends from there. Community means any relationship, from two people to a large organization. A productive community is a set of relationships where synergy lives, where collective good and individual good are *one*.

With a clear focus on value-creation, change and growth are more readily embraced. This embracement of growth occurs throughout the alliance. Embracement of growth is love; it is actually the loving of love. This evolving-while-growing model is called "bounded instability" – the traditional hierarchal organization provides the bounds; the alliance is consciously unstable. A growth-orientation causes disruptive changes, first in the alliance, and then in the greater business.

As we become more focused on accomplishing an alliance's collective vision, our traditional roles in the business' hierarchy become less important. Individuals become increasingly passionate about the alliance's purpose. With this shared vision, perception of self and the organization changes. While retaining our traditional hierarchical roles that we inherited from the business, we become adaptive and flexible in accomplishing the results of the alliance.

Some Spiritual Practices in Strategic Alliancing

Even the role of leader changes as situations dictate. We are more focused on results than titles. We are focused on principles more than personalities.

The members of this community become increasingly "inner directed and other focused." They are concerned about personal integrity. They continually go within to draw closer to truth and deal with their own integrity issues. With this inner honesty the community gains trust via healthy confrontation. Issues are quickly addressed, not suppressed. This is for the good of the alliance.

Truth is sought out, even if the process leads to intense confrontation. Individuals know that their success is directly linked to community success. Individualistic, self-centered behavior focused solely on personal success at the expense of community is toxic in an alliance. This behavior must be confronted in a loving manner for the sake of community. At times the best thing for the community may be for someone to leave; this may even include the alliance manager.

As an alliance manager our role is to be the servant to the alliance. We are about reminding others of our valued vision, and we work to remove obstacles impeding that value. We help management understand how they can also be servants to the alliance. We are willing to give them direction in order to help us achieve our vision.

An alliance team that has become a productive community becomes a place where "ordinary people accomplish extraordinary results." Such a place attracts collaboration – collaborative people and a collaborative climate.

Transforming an Alliance into a Productive Community – *Practical Steps*

1. Have a clear, integrated vision of Self (from Chapter 5) and a clear, holistic integrative vision of the alliance (from the 2-Slide Methodology™ in *Focus Collective Attention on Value*). Then personally embody and continually extend this passionate vision throughout the alliance.

2. Be the source of empowerment in the alliance. Empower

others via the practice of *Self-Obsolescence*. Be "the ruthless hero" of the alliance.

3. Envision the alliance as a productive community, a place which attracts success, where people feel "a part of," and where extraordinary results are natural. Alliances face unusual challenges, primarily from their own business; for our success we need to embody the change that is needed, starting within.

4. Given the unusual challenges we face, we need to embrace an unusual form. We need to create a productive community.

5. Seek the truth. Share the truth. Be willing to be confrontational, for the sake of individual and collective growth. Remember, loving confrontation was covered in both *Be Lovingly Confrontational* (primarily about problems) and *Focus Collective Attention on Value* (primarily about greatness).

6. Willingly face fears - in self and in others. We all have fears of change and fear of the unknown. Realize that our deepest fears are around success, not failure. Patiently and lovingly help others confront and work through their deep-seated fears.[141]

7. Do not allow individuals in the alliance to be constrained by business' hierarchical structure or systems. Think "outside the hierarchical box." The phrase "That is not my job" does not work in an alliance. "How can *we* get that done?" does work. Principles dictate that we focus on "what is the right thing to do," rather than on traditional expectations, rewards or punishment.

8. Remain tough on issues but soft on people. Embody and expect excellence in a deeply empathetic and loving manner. Be ready and willing to attract success and repulse mediocrity.

9. Be willing to see people naturally come and go as you and the

alliance evolve and grow. Be willing to accept the idea that in time *you* may be the one who has to leave your alliance, for the greater good – yours and the collective's.[142]

Transforming an Alliance into a Productive Community – *Spiritual Basis*

- **Oneness** – community.

- **Love** – growth, the stuff that "glues us together." The greatness that is all around us and in us, if we are bold enough to overcome our fear of success. The greatness that *is* us.

- **We Create** – focus collective attention on value, removal of impediments, and a vision of productive community for the alliance's form.

Transforming an Alliance into a Productive Community – *Benefits*

- Fun and **enjoyment** – more fun than one person deserves!

- A greater sense of **purpose**, an integrated life where we love our work and work our love.

- Greater **success** – in every way.

A productive community is not normal in traditional business. But alliances are not traditional. We need a new form; we need a new home. We all seek for such a home, a place of love, acceptance and growth. This is a vision for how human relationships are *supposed* to *work*. Home is about acceptance and embracement; it is …

… that place where we find the peace and harmony that comes from learning to live with the knowledge of our own imperfections and from learning to accept the imperfections of others. Such a place, such a home, can exist in various settings, but its ultimate foundation rests jointly within self and within some group of trusted others. Some places are more conducive to this experience than others. But wherever and whenever we

> *do attain that sense of being-at-home, we experience a falling away of tensions, a degree of balance between the pushing and pulling forces of our lives. In such a place, we can cease fighting – most importantly, we can cease fighting with ourselves. We find the space to be the imperfect beings that we are, and we discover that in such a space, we also become able to let others be who they are.*
>
> *- The Spirituality of Imperfection*
> by Ernest Kutz & Katherine Ketcham

In such a grounding home we have the means to "face the unknown and walk naked into the land of uncertainty," knowing things will work out and great success lies ahead.

Be the Metaphor for Metamorphosis – *be* the change

Change starts with us; it starts within us.

Be the Metaphor for Metamorphosis – *Situation*

How can we affect change in our alliance, particularly where there are deficiencies, such as:

- low trust
- poor communication
- a lack of productivity – low value-creation
- a negative environment

Be the Metaphor for Metamorphosis – *Basic Ideas*

Through *Presence*, *Awareness* and *Focusing Collective Attention on Value*, understand what is needed in the alliance. What change

Some Spiritual Practices in Strategic Alliancing

is needed? Then – *be* the change needed in the alliance. As within, so without; always, *first* go within.

Be the change you want to see in the world.
- Mahatma Gandhi

If greater trust is needed, first trust your Self by confronting your own internal integrity gaps. Know yourself and be true to your Self. Then confront external issues; confront the issue of low trust. Create and embrace confrontational situations which call for trust, and trust will come.

If more open communication is needed, be more open. Work on increasing presence and awareness. Be open, bold and deep in communications. Lovingly stir things up.

If greater value is needed, *be* of greater value. Be of service. Give and receive. Practice self-obsolescence.

Seek the truth and shine your light on the greatness you discover. Choose to look past the negative and focus collective attention on solutions and the positive. This is not to say we should ignore the negative; deal with it and move on.

We affect positive change in unspoken and unspeakable ways as we change and grow:

When you find the way others will find you.
Passing by on the road they will be drawn to your door.
The way that cannot be heard will be echoed in your voice.
The way that cannot be seen will be reflected in your eyes.

- Lao-tzu in *Tao-te Ching*

It Is All About Relationship – the spirit's home

Spirituality is about *deepening* relationships, because spirit lives *in* relationships.

> *The Holy Spirit's temple is not a body, but a relationship.*
> - A Course in Miracles

Spirit resides *in* relationship, in *the between*, in *the midst*. Spirit lives:

- between people – "when two or more are gathered …"
- between us and the Infinite (or higher power, the Universe, nature, … the something else)
- between us and ourselves – *between* the silent observer (our true Self) and the observed (our thoughts, the world around us)
- between *ideas* – a third option that exists *between* two different ideas, beyond simple compromise
- between companies – the answers, problems and answers to the problems all lie *in* the alliance

Spirituality deepens relationship, and with a deepening of relationship we grow spiritually. This is a virtuous cycle. We embody this virtuous cycle; we become the "eye of the hurricane." With our intense serenity we bring purpose, direction and vision into our chaotic world of alliancing.

This chapter has introduced a few spiritual practices helpful in deepening relationship and increasing the value-creating effectiveness in an alliance. There are surely other practices. This is simply a start.

9. Conclusion – A Call to Action – Be Focused, Be Bold, Be …

The evolution of this book has itself been an exercise in *oneness* – this book is "a we thing." It started with the experience of one alliance manager, someone who sought to understand the *fundamentals* in strategic alliances. Over 15 years the ideas in this book have evolved, with feedback and input from many others. Thoughts and encouragement came from colleagues, friends, family members, experienced strategic alliance managers and consultants – other spiritual beings.[143]

This book talks about spiritual principles, simple truths. Truth can be parsed, described and explained using a vast variety of words and from diverse perspectives based on a wide range of personal experiences. The author claims no monopoly on truth or how to describe it. There are surely other simple truths beyond those discussed in Chapter 6, which when held in consciousness, help us grow, as well as grow closer to one another. There are other spiritual practices, beyond those mentioned in Chapter 8, which authentically deepen relationships and transform alliances.

I do claim that spirituality deepens relationships and improves alliances. I do claim that spirituality is directly relevant and urgently needed in alliances today.

Spirituality Addresses Root Cause of Alliance Failure

Over half of all strategic alliances fail to achieve their expected value. Forty percent of these failures are due to poor relationships. In general, businesses fail at the art and science of healthy relationships.

Spirituality uses practical principles, here and now, in order to deepen relationships. And deeper is always better. Spirituality addresses the nontraditional cause for alliance failures – a lack in relationship.

Alliancing is hard work. Living by spiritual principles is also hard work. Both types of work call for boldness, persistence and tenacity. When we create a situation that "calls" for certain things, certain personal attributes, those things will come. We can always use more boldness, persistence and tenacity. Why not call for these things through the embodiment of bold value-creating ideas? Be the change.

Summary: simplicity, relationship, presence & awareness, attitude & mindset, love

Here are a few key ideas in this book – some "take aways":

- **Simplicity** takes us toward truth – look for and use simplicity. The simple truths of *oneness, now, we are divine, we create* and *love* help deepen relationships. Hold these simple truths in consciousness.

- **Relationship** – spirituality deepens relationship (with others, Self and the Infinite). Spirit lives *in* a relationship – right there *in between*. The opportunities, insights, problems and answers to those problems lie in relationships – in the between – *in the midst*.

- **Presence & awareness** – the starting point for awakening and spiritual growth. Start here and continually revisit presence and awareness. Live a meditative, mindful life. Be fully aware of what is going on within, around and among us. Where are you?

- **Attitude & mindset** is the most important stuff for us to work on, but we cannot work on this stuff alone. We need trusted others. Connect. Be part of. Life is "a we thing." Attitude & mindset starts with our perspective toward our Self. Who do you think you are?

- **Love** is all there is. There is only love and the absence of love, or fear. Love is synonymous with growth. Love is the universal force which counters entropy (decay) and compels us all to grow: individuals, organizations, companies, countries and mankind. Our choice really boils down "grow or die." Goodness and greatness prevail. Do we choose to perceive only greatness?

And when you work with love you bind your Self to yourself, and to one another, and to God.
- *The Prophet* by Kahlil Gibran

As we practice simple spiritual truths, our attitude & mindset improves, naturally leading us toward more authentic and effective behavior. Relationships deepen and improve as we embody a more loving and growth-oriented perspective. We transform our alliance as we transform ourselves.

Be the Metaphor for Metamorphosis

Be the change you want to see in the world.
- Mahatma Gandhi

Be the change that is needed in your alliance. Be present and aware enough to notice the alliance's needs. Does it need greater trust or more open communication? If so, embody those changes. Be the greatness in you in order to help bring out the greatness in others. Be the light. Shine on! "As we let our own light shine, we unconsciously give other people permission to do the same. As we are liberated from our own fear, our presence automatically liberates others."[144]

Living this way calls for bold courageousness. Those attributes will grow within you.

If Not Us, Who? If Not Now, When?

The highly *competitive*, fear-based, "me vs. you" climate in business actually stifles business' growth. There is a better way. We don't have to keep living like this.

Spiritual Principles in Strategic Alliances

Our job is to help make *collaboration* occur in business, resulting in creating greater value. Who else better than strategic alliance managers to show business the way? Who else better to embody the practical value of simple spiritual truths? We work in an area of business where spirituality is strategically needed and where the practical results will be immediately apparent.

We have the answers. You have the answers within *you*. I am simply stirring up thoughts and asking deep questions in order to help surface those solutions and insights.

Refer back to Figure 2.4 – *Are we begging for help? If not, why not?!* The story of the beggar that began in Chapter 2 continues:

"Ever look inside?" asked the stranger. "No," said the beggar, "what's the point? There's nothing in there." "Have a look inside," insisted the stranger. Together they managed to pry open the lid. With astonishment, disbelief and elation, they saw that the box was filled with great treasure.

- *The Power of Now* by Eckhart Tolle (paraphrased)

Figure 9.4 – The answer lies *within*. *We* find it together.

Conclusion

Such is the treasure we each have *within*. But paradoxically, we cannot get to that treasure by ourselves. We need each other.

Notice some interesting details when comparing Figures 2.4 and 9.4. The process of going within changed the beggar. Can you see how he has changed? Also, both guys are actually the same guy, symbolizing our oneness and symbolizing a sense of timelessness; perhaps the stranger is reaching back in time to help his younger self. The stranger is more awake and cleaner, further down the path of spiritual awakening. The stranger wears glasses, symbolizing that he has a different perspective. These illustrations are emblematic of both oneness and timelessness. The stranger is lovingly reaching back in time to help another along the path of growth.

Metaphorically, I am writing to myself 15-20 years ago. I am writing to give freely of my best ideas to you. In the writing and publishing of this book I am striving to obsolete myself.

May these ideas have a transformational impact in you and on your alliance. My deepest hope is that these ideas get extended, in quality and in depth. Ideas grow as they get extended to others. Ideas grow by sharing. If you'd like to share some of your ideas with the author, please send e-mail to **joe@spibr.org**.

Over time we will establish a venue and mechanism for collectively sharing our ideas, leading toward a productive value-enabling community. This community will be focused on the practical application of spiritual principles to improve business relationships. Check out **www.SPiBR.org** for updates.

Suggested Daily Top Fives

Below are suggested **principles** (things to *think*) and **practices** (things to *do*) to be the metaphor for metamorphosis and transform status quo mediocrity into greatness – **first in self**, then in your alliance.

5 Principles (things to *think*)	5 Practices (things to *do*)
• **Oneness** – hear the voice of the collective; see others as Self	• **Be Lovingly Confrontational** – shine your light with love and precision
• **Now** – be fully present in each holy instant of time, one eternal now	• **Focus Collective Attention** – focus and refocus on value and impediments
• **We Are Divine** – see the divine in all; see all relationships as sacred and eternal	• **Self-Obsolescence** – give freely your greatest ideas; giving and receiving are one
• **We Create** – thought is causal; see loving thoughts as light; be very mindful	• **Be an Illuminating Mirror** – shine your light into another; reflect their light back to them
• **Love** – the universal force compelling growth; goodness is inevitable; be "in love"	• **Be the Metaphor for Metamorphosis** – be the change that is needed

Be the change.

10. Appendix

Key Terms

Below are clarifications of a few important words used in this book.

Ego: the basis for one of two fundamentally different thought systems (the other is based on spirit).[145] Thoughts or perspectives based on *separation*, "me vs. you," and fear – separation from others, the Infinite and even Self. Grounded in a *lack of presence* – we are not in the present moment. We feel bad about the past and fear the future.

Fear: a lack or absence of love, leading to other feelings based in a sense of lack, like anger. Fear can be exhibited as defensiveness and attack, trying to prove one is right and another wrong.

Grandeur: accepting and embracing the greatness in us all. Grandeur is not grandiosity, which is grounded in ego, especially "me vs. you." Grandeur is about looking at how great *we* are. Grandiosity is about look how great *I* am - how I am greater than you.

Love: primarily synonymous with growth. Love is the universal force countering entropy or decay. The force of love compels us all to grow.

Love is the will to extend one's self for the purpose of nurturing one's own or another's spiritual growth.
- *The Road Less Traveled* by M. Scott Peck

Think deeply about this universal force which compels growth, which is the Infinite and is good, which is in us and among us. Love has some interesting attributes: forgiveness, happiness, creativity, growth, health, enthusiasm, light, peace, intelligence, kindness, relationship, power, beauty, purpose, abundance, joy, spirit, reverence, acceptance, non-judgment, inspiration, enlightenment, timelessness, charity, patience, service, awe, affection, esteem, respect, presence, optimism, purpose – all pointing to the Great I Am within each of us, the core truth within.[146]

There is only love or the absence of love; and the answer is always love:

Where there is love, your brother must give it to you because of what it is. But where there is a call for love, you must give it because of what you are.

- A Course in Miracles

Given love is a force compelling all to grow, the term "tough love" is actually a redundant statement.

Mind: synonymous with "the silent observer" or our awareness.[147] Our mind looks through either the clouded lens of ego and fear, or the clearly illuminating lens of spirit and love. In each instant of time, it is one or the other – ego or spirit – fear or love.

Spirit: the basis for one of two fundamentally different thought systems (the other is based on ego). Spirit includes thoughts or perspectives based on *connectedness*, life as "a we thing," and love. We feel deeply connected with others, the Infinite and Self. Grounded in a *sense of presence* – it's easy to be very present, knowing that now is the only time when change or growth can occur.

Truth: is true. Truth rings true within, based on experience. Simplicity leads us toward truth. We see immediate practical benefits as we draw closer to and embody truth. Words become less and less useful as we get closer to core truth. There are various ways to describe truth, but the words we choose are simply signposts to be used while helpful and then discarded.

Appendix

Sometimes the best way to recognize truth is indirectly. Sometimes we can see truth working in others' lives better than they can see it, and better than we can see it in ours. And sometimes others can see truth working in our life better than we can.

Value: an expanded and nontraditional notion of value beyond just incremental sales revenue. We should be *especially* focused on long-term and *intangible forms* of value, the forms most often missed by traditional business planning processes. Often the intangible forms of value exceed tangible forms in overall value to a company.

It is today's intangible and timeless forms of value that will lead to tomorrow's tangible value.

As a starting point, here is a fairly expansive list of value to think about:

- mutual growth
- profitable incremental revenue
- access to new markets
- business process innovation
- risk-mitigation
- increased brand recognition
- improved strategic plans
- improved partner loyalty
- knowledge transfer
- increased market share
- development of new markets
- reduction of competitive threat
- risk-sharing
- brand loyalty
- additional strategic options
- increased customer loyalty
- new organizational capabilities
- increased market penetration
- improved time-to-market
- neutralization of competitive threat
- diversification of product portfolio
- improved customer satisfaction
- increased employee loyalty

Books Along My Path

> *Then I found my head one day when I wasn't even trying.*
> *And here I have to say, 'cause there is no use in lying, lying,*
> *Yes the answer lies within, so why not take a look now?*
> *Kick out the devil's sin, pick up, pick up a good book now.*
> — Cat Stevens, in the song *On the Road to Find Out*

From 2003 through 2005, I took 30-40 spiritual books to Heidelberg, Germany to read and reflect upon. During this time I was living half-time in Heidelberg and establishing the HP/SAP enterprise printing alliance. Below is a list of especially impactful books on my journey to apply spirituality in alliancing (listed in the rough chronological order in which they were read):

- *The Bible*
- *The Prophet* by Kahlil Gibran
- *The Road Less Traveled* by M. Scott Peck, M.D.
- *Getting to Yes: Negotiating Agreement Without Giving In* by Roger Fisher, William Ury and Bruce Patton (in Program on Negotiation course at Harvard, MIT & Tufts Universities)
- *Emotional Intelligence: Why it can matter more than IQ* by Daniel Goleman
- *Alcoholics Anonymous*, A.A. World Services Inc.
- *Narcotics Anonymous*, NAWS, Inc.
- *Sermon on the Mount* by Emmet Fox
- *The Spirituality of Imperfection: Storytelling and the Search for Meaning* by Ernest Kurtz and Katherine Ketcham
- *Loving-Kindness: The Revolutionary Art of Happiness* by Sharon Salzberg
- *The Power of Now: A Guide to Spiritual Enlightenment* by Eckhart Tolle

Appendix

- *There's a Spiritual Solution to Every Problem* by Wayne Dyer
* *A Return to Love: Reflections on the Principles of A Course in Miracles* by Marianne Williamson
* *Change the World: How Ordinary People Can Accomplish Extraordinary Results* by Robert E Quinn
* *A Course in Miracles,* Foundation for Inner Peace
- *The Corporate Mystic: a guidebook for visionaries with their feet on the ground* by Gay Hendricks and Kate Ludeman

("*" denotes a "top 5 list" – especially impactful)

Other publications written by the author:

- *The Role of Strategic Alliance Manager: a unique, holistic and empowering perspective* (the 3x3 Role Methodology™) available at **www.spibr.org/strategic_alliance_mgmt.pdf**.

- *Simply Focus on Incremental Value and Value-Impediments: transforming a strategic alliance through simplicity* (the 2-Slide Methodology™) available at **www.spibr.org/2-slide_methodology.pdf**.

- *Building Trust in Strategic Alliances: enabling greater value* – selected as an ASAP Best Practice (**www.strategic-alliances.org**), available at **www.spibr.org/Building_trust_and_value_in_alliances.pdf**.

Spiritual Principles in Strategic Alliances

Thoughts on Metrics

Here are thoughts on job or personal performance metrics.

What we look at, changes. Focused attention is causal – it affects us and the world around us.

Metrics is a challenging field of work. We need to be very careful about what and how we measure. Be careful about what we do with the measurements. This is not an exhaustive treatise on job metrics or alliance performance metrics. As in other areas of this book, this section is intended to get us focused on the core issues, in self and in the alliance, and to stir up thoughts.

Here is a list of suggested areas where job performance metrics might be developed. Clearly, these metrics should be developed collaboratively between alliance manager and his/her manager. Alliance-wide discussions with others may also be helpful.

Initially, focus on a few simple, obvious core metrics. Then, later, expand and learn by doing.

1. **Improving attitude & mindset** – jointly define key attitudes & mindsets specific to the industry, company, alliance and phase of development (consider the success-oriented insights discussed in the last two sections of Chapter 4 – *The Insightful Intersect* and *Summary*, and the *Simple Fundamental Truths* in Chapter 6, to start)

    a. **in self** – self-knowledge, *be the change*

        i. having a clear, unambiguous and bold job description – for self, manager and others

        ii. being self-correcting and willing to receive feedback from others – especially around negative, value-inhibiting behaviors – willingness to honestly go within to examine motives and integrity gaps

        iii. being mindful – having a deep, loving meditative presence

    b. **in others** – assess and encourage – no matter the problem, the answer is always love

i. dealing positively with unhealthy behaviors in others – practice loving confrontation
  ii. call out others and self on "yeah but" addictions: drama, complexity, etc.
  iii. inspire others to be better people
c. improve the **collaborative climate** in the alliance – be aware
  i. fear vs. love based assessment
  ii. trust
     1. risk-taking
  iii. communication
     1. clear and simple
     2. audience appropriate
     3. just-enough and just-in-time
  iv. a productive community
  v. healthy confrontation
     1. clear understanding of value-impediments with practical recommendations for overcoming them
  vi. sense of vision or purposeful direction
     1. clear understanding of the incremental-value potential in the alliance
     2. long-term and intangible forms of value
d. embodying and encouraging <u>positive behaviors</u> – jointly define
  i. continual transformation – e.g., lead alliance through create-divide-create phases
2. **Deepening relationship** – how will this get assessed? Surveys? Interviews? Continually!
  a. **with Self** - integrity

b. **with others** – openness and inclusiveness
c. **between others** – open, trustful, deep discussions
d. **between the companies** – sense of community – healthy confrontation
e. **between *ideas*** – creative brainstorming
f. embodying and encouraging **relationship-deepening behaviors** – jointly define

3. **Skills** – jointly define key skills – traditional and nontraditional skills, especially the relevant *relationship-ization* of *people*, *alliance-ization* of *their work*
   a. **relationship**-improving skills
      i. ability to assess fit
   b. **personal** development
      i. negotiating
   c. **training others**
      i. relationship-ization of people
      ii. alliance-ization of their work

4. **Knowledge** – jointly defined based on unique needs: legal, regulatory, finance, strategic, etc.
   a. personal acquisition
   b. dissemination to others

Damaging metrics – "wrong-headed" measures that negatively affect the health/climate in alliance:

a. Get the **deal at all costs**. *Must win* attitude that fosters "rape, pillage and burn" behaviors.
b. Focusing *only* on **near-term incremental sales revenue** and holding the alliance manager **singularly responsible** for its accomplishment. This ignores longer-term and intangible forms of value. And this places the alliance manager in a position where he cannot apply spiritual principles (i.e., it is all about "me").

c. Metrics focused *only* on **alliance manager's organizational home.** Not allowing the alliance manager to be holistic and embrace the entire business as necessary to accomplish the alliance's objectives. This is an artificial constraint often counter to the partner's interests.

d. Metrics developed for the **internal stakeholders who most influence personal direct-line manager.** Excessively driven by politics, not by what is best for the alliance or the overall business.

e. **Constantly changing** metrics tied to "strategy de jour." Institutionalized inconsistency and chaos.

Thoughts on Meditation

> *All of man's miseries derive from*
> *not being able to sit quietly in a room alone.*
> — Blaise Pascal – French scientist,
> mathematician and philosopher

Simply an exercise

Simplicity fosters spiritual growth. Simple concepts are impactful, such as "giving and receiving are one" or "the temple of the spirit is a relationship." We can often make simple things complex, even meditation.

Meditation is simply *an exercise of the mind*, for practical benefit, in every area of life. During meditation we become more mindful (aware of our thoughts), more present (here and now), and more connected. We connect with the light, truth and love within. This deepens our connectedness with the Infinite, others and Self (the divine essence within us and between us).

> *We can make our minds so like still water that beings gather*
> *about us, that they may see their own images,*
> *and so live for a moment with a clearer,*
> *perhaps even with a fiercer life because of our quiet.*
> — William Butler Yeats

Practical benefits from meditating

As we become more aware of our thoughts, as we become more conscious (awake), we access deeper and more expansive creativity. We gain more control over our thoughts. Thought *is causal*. So, we gain increasing control over our lives and the world around us. This may sound like arrogant grandiosity; it is actually *self-full grandeur* (neither selfless nor selfish – but full-of-Self).

As we become increasingly aware of and in control of our

thoughts, we are able to assess and change our attitude & mindset. Change in attitude & mindset is accomplished through a change in perspective, from fear-based to love-based thoughts. We change our view of others and situations. Remember, we are working on drawing closer to Self (our divine essence, which involves others – life is "a we thing").

We gain increased presence, evidenced when we look within and see serenity. This intense presence affects others and situations, increasing our effectiveness, often in unspoken ways. As we connect more deeply within to spirit and love, that depth of connectedness increases in every aspect of life. We have deeper, more meaningful, and more impactful relationships with others.

This concept of connectedness can often encompass time – we begin to connect the dots with a timelessness of perspective. This timelessness ends up circling back; providing us with patience, persistence and tenacity. We begin to see a natural flow of events around us, heading toward an end-point vision, which we know will be accomplished – it is "simply a matter of time."

How to meditate

You know. Trust your Self.

The point of meditation is to connect with the truth and light within you. Why not accept and use that truth from the very start? Consider some of the thoughts below, listen to others, read books; but know that you know what is right for you. Stay true to that truth within you. Use some ideas; discard the rest.

Just do it. Set aside 15-20 minutes of quiet uninterrupted time – sometimes more, sometimes less. Meditate every day, at least once – some times more often. Simply sit down and be quiet. Be still. Be.

Be comfortable. Either sit or lie down, you know what is right for you. But mediation is not a nap. Relax and consume less air. Be conscious of each breath – be aware of each instant of time within each breath.

Observe your thoughts. In *The Power of Now,* Eckhart Tolle describes our spirit as the silent observer – so observe. Our egoic mind does not like to be watched.[148] As we sit quietly and simply observe our thoughts, we will notice our thoughts simply fade away. Observation, alone, is quieting. Do not think about your thoughts – for that is just another thought. Observe. Be the observer. From breath to breath, in each holy instant of time, simply watch your thoughts.

Sometimes in meditation we may choose to direct our thoughts toward others or specific situations in our lives. In *Loving-Kindness* Sharon Salzberg writes about "metta," translated as "love" or "loving-kindness."

The spirit of metta is unconditional: open and unobstructed.
Like water poured from one vessel to another,
metta flows freely, taking the shape of each situation
without changing [love's] essence.

As you imagine yourself pouring your love into another vessel, imagine yourself breathing in love and then breathing out love – toward another person or into situations in your life. Then, over time, see how those relationships grow and deepen. Observe.

As you deeply connect with the light and love within, feel your entire body with each breath. Eckhart Tolle talks about one portal into the unmanifested (spirit) being the intense feeling of our entire body. As you breathe in love, observe that feeling. As you breathe out love, observe that feeling. Feel the flow of love with every fiber of your body – be.

In each instant, and in every breath – observe – be.

In time you will attract people, books and situations which will help you advance your meditative practice. An enlightened phrase is, "When the student is really ready she will realize the teacher is with her always and everywhere." Observe this teaching. Then select and use what is true for you and discard the rest.

These are a few thoughts on meditation. The critical points are (a) just do it, and (b) you know.

Appendix

A meditative life

Exercising our mind will help in every area of life. We will have greater presence in our relationships. We will become more mindful and creative in our work.

Time will change. We will become more patient and persistent as we gain a timelessness of perspective. But, paradoxically, we may become impatient when others do not see the same timeless vision we do.

As we draw closer to the intense and loving light within, our lives become more intense. We will be more comfortable in intense situations, realizing those situations do not define us. Our serene intensity will attract others into our life.

> *When you find the way others will find you.*
> *Passing by on the road they will be drawn to your door.*
> *The way that cannot be heard will be echoed in your voice.*
> *The way that cannot be seen will be reflected in your eyes.*
> — Lao-tzu in *Tao-te Ching*

Just do it. Be more connected, grounded and centered. Be more in the flow and more creative.

Be still and know. Be still. Be.

Thoughts on Two Thought Systems

Would you be hostage to the ego or host to [the spirit]? Let this question be asked ... every time you make a decision.[149]

— *A Course in Miracles*

This section makes a bold statement:

Our thoughts are *always* grounded in *one* of only two thought systems – from moment to moment, in each instant of time, we are either:

- in ego and fear

or

- in spirit and love

You might consider this black and white thinking, overly-simplistic and not reflective of real life. At the end of this section a couple of models are suggested for how our thoughts might get averaged over time, leading to a consideration of how duality vs. loss of duality is linked to the nature of love, and the Infinite.

The practical purpose of this section is to make us more acutely aware of our thoughts. Thought is causal; it is where creativity resides. Thought *is* creativity. Thought is where *authentic behavior* originates. How are we directing causality? We begin by noticing what we are thinking. Notice whether our thoughts are grounded in love or fear. Notice how our lives are directly influenced by the cumulative effect of our chosen thoughts. Become aware of our moment-to-moment selection of thought system.

The point of all this is to *wake up*.

In each instant of time – it is only within an instant of time (this moment) that growth occurs. The *unhealthy* use of time is our greatest obstacle in changing ourselves. When we feel bad about the past (shame or guilt) or when we are fearful of the future, we remain stuck. Shame, guilt and fear *distract* us from the present moment; they distract us from the only point in time when change can occur. Consequently, the past gets reflected into the future and we do not grow. It is hard to consciously remember that we cannot change the past and the future is not here.

In order to transform ourselves and the world around us we must stay present, we must be conscious of our thoughts and choose to *change* our thoughts.

Hostage of the ego or host to the spirit – the table below illustrates how our chosen thought system makes itself evident.[150] Look at how we respond to situations, how we manage information, how we deal with others, how we see life and our use of time.

Before we change our thoughts, we need to know what they are.

In each instant of time, are we …

… Hostage of the Ego?	… Host to the Spirit?
Situations	
Scarcity or zero-sum mindset – fixed resources – "your win is my loss" – we are "*dividing* a pie."	**Abundance** mindset – limitless resources – "we create value" – we are "*expanding* a pie."
In problematic situations: focus on **judging & punishing** – make someone *responsible*.	In problematic situations: focus on thoroughly **understanding** – then are *we* able to *respond*.
Information	
Secrets – *hoard* information to *keep* power.	**Openness** – *share* information to *create* power.
Complexity – *analyze* to great detail – lose sight of the forest for the trees – cloud simple truths.	**Simplicity** – uncover to *simple insights* – sees holistic trends – asks simple but tough questions.
Others	
Life is all about "**me**" – me *vs.* you; and me *vs.* the world. Roles and *titles* are important.	Life is all about "**we**" – me *with* the world. Our aligned *intent* is paramount.
Either **selfish** or **self-less**; both are focused on *separation*.	Focused on **Self-fullness**; grandeur through our *oneness* and aligned intent.
Conflict – excessive competitiveness – alienates and distances self from others.	**Confrontation** – seeks solutions and growth – faces difficult issues – high rapport and high trust.

Spiritual Principles in Strategic Alliances

... Hostage of the Ego?	... Host to the Spirit?
Grandiosity – I must prove *I* am superior.	**Grandeur** – you & I are grand; *we* are invincible.
Life	
A **segregated life**. Behavior *varies* based on specific areas of life (work, home, etc.).	An **integrated life**. *Consistency* of behavior across all areas of life. We work our love.
A pervading sense of **separation**. Separated from others. Separated from the spirit within.	A sense of **connectedness** or oneness of us all. At one with Self, connected with spirit. At peace.
Fear – fear of others, fear of failure and **fear of success**. A mundane state of *mediocrity*.	**Love** – love of life, love of others, love of Self and love of love. Fearlessly embrace *success*.
Time	
Obsessed with **time** – feels guilty about the past, fearful of future. Distracted (not present). Over-booked calendar and proud of it – "I am too busy."	**Timelessness** – realizes that each instant is all we ever have. Focused on doing the "next right thing." Presence interwoven with goals – vision.

Note that the distinctions between ego and spirit, or between fear and love, are often subtle but significant (e.g., grandiosity vs. grandeur or conflict vs. confrontation). The key issues are around separation vs. connectedness. What is our sense of peace within? What are our motives?

Cumulative effect of our thoughts – most of us don't live "black and white lives" like these two thought systems suggest; if we did we might seek out psychiatric help. Normally life is experienced as relatively smooth ebbs and flows. Rather than harshly disruptive black and white swings, we generally experience transitions through shades of grey – in between black and white. So, perhaps it is through time-averaging that our lives are smoothed from black and white into cyclical shades of grey.

Appendix

If there is an Opposite of Love …

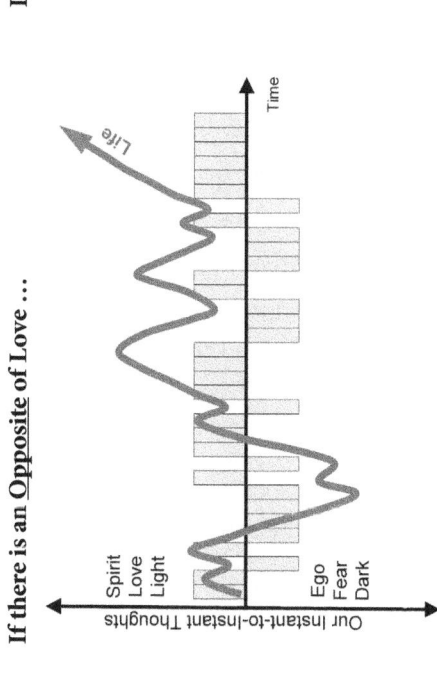

… then:

- We either progress or we digress, there is no "standing still." Either up or down.
- We can experience valleys or troughs, "back sliding."
- This seems to suggest a duality, a world of opposites, where God/love/spirit has an opposite (i.e., not an all-powerful or all-loving God).
- This model seems to generate fear. Which seems to suggest this line of thinking is itself grounded in ego.

If there is only an Absence of Love …

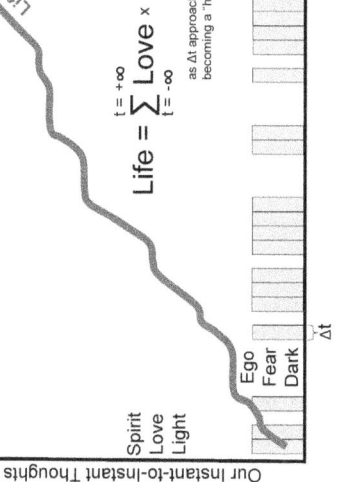

$$\text{Life} = \sum_{t=-\infty}^{t=+\infty} \text{Love} \times \Delta t$$

as Δt approaches 0, becoming a 'holy instant'

… then:

- We either progress or we plateau (stagnate).
- Given that love is a force which compels us to grow, plateaus may effectively *feel* like valleys, as life (the *flow* caused by love) seems to "pass us by."
- This seems to suggest an all-loving God who only wants us to grow.
- This model seems more loving. This model is also simpler, and, therefore, perhaps truer.
- All instances of loving thought are good. All of our loving moments add up to make our life what it is today. (Ref: the formula – life is the summation of all instances of love, from negative infinity to positive infinity, as delta t approach 0, or as we "stay in the moment.")

209

There *is* a time-averaging effect that our moment-to-moment thoughts have on our lives. As we awaken to our thoughts, as we become more mindful and live a more meditative life, we become aware of the cumulative impact our thoughts have on the world around us.

What are the practical implications?

- Realize the powerful impact that our loving thoughts have on our lives.
- Be more awake or more aware of our moment-to-moment thoughts.

Dealing with it in ourselves – how can we deal with our own thoughts? Below are some suggestions. These ideas are related to the simple truths that now (this instant in time) is all we ever have, and we should strive to stay very present:

1. **Be aware.** Continually *observe* our thoughts. Be mindful, live a meditative life. This sounds easy because it is simple; but it is hard work calling for continual awareness.

2. **Ask, "What am I thinking?"** Throughout the day ask this question, especially when we sense fear.

3. **Ask ourselves about the basis for our thoughts.** Are our thoughts based in fear, scarcity, separation, isolation, self-will and competition? Or are they grounded in love, abundance, connectedness, a sense of oneness, others and collaboration? This self-observation grows over time.

4. **Ask others.** Life is a "we thing" (an alliance). We need the help of others to *see* more clearly our own thoughts. Develop and nurture invaluable high-trust relationships. Seek out honest feedback.

5. **Relationships with others.** Based on our oneness there is a direct correlation between internal relationships (with Self and spirit) and external relationships (with others). When everyone around us starts "turning into assholes," it is a sign of lack within. It is that poverty within that needs to be "dealt with."

Appendix

Helping others

When we think we see evidences of ego-based, fear-based or scarcity-based thinking in others, we are faced with an insightful opportunity. The suggestions below will take you deeply within. These suggestions also remind us of our oneness, and that life is "a we thing."

1. **Don't "join them."** If someone's thought system is ego- or fear-based, their perceptions are legitimized (made real) when another "joins them" in their belief in separateness, scarcity and fear. If you retaliate for something they have done, you confirm that their egoic, fear-based perspectives are "true" – at least at that point in time and in that relationship. Therefore, *simply* choose not to join them in their "game" of fear, separateness and scarcity.

2. **Stay grounded in spirit and love.** We can choose to see the other person as the divine being they are. We can see the situation as a tremendous opportunity for us to embody love and facilitate growth. Be prepared for growth to occur for all concerned – for you and others. "Fasten your seatbelt!"

3. **Help them perceive differently.** As we stay grounded in spirit and love, we are inspired as to what to do, and more importantly what NOT to do. Perhaps we simply stay present for them – maintaining a loving presence and assertively listen. Perhaps we need to confront a difficult issue in the relationship, knowing that if this confrontation is done right and in love, it will change perceptions – yours and theirs.

4. **Join them in the spirit/loving thought system.** With a changed perspective we can join them in the spirit- or love-based thought system and make that thought system real for others and for us. We can consciously express and acknowledge our gratitude for them as individuals, help them see their own divine nature (sometimes that's hard for us to see and remember).[151] We can openly talk about the transcendence and transformation that occurred in the relationship – that's OK – that's good – heck, that's great!

> *The answer that I give my brother is what I am asking for. And what I learn of him is what I learn about myself.*
> - A Course in Miracles

If others are in fear, we love them. If others are angry, we love them. If they are in love, we love them. The answer is always, love.

A belief in separation, which the ego promotes, leads naturally to fear-based thinking and a scarcity mentality. Love leads naturally to an abundance mindset.

> *Littleness and glory are the choices open to your striving and your vigilance. You will always choose one at the expense of the other.*
>
> *Would you be hostage to the ego or host to [the spirit]? Let this question be asked ... every time you make a decision.*
> - A Course in Miracles

Appendix

Thoughts on Time

Time is an enigma. Scientists cannot explain time. They cannot explain why it is that time exists in only one dimension. Why we can remember the past but not the future? What is the smallest measure of time?

In our lives, time is also enigmatic. We wrestle with time. Are we using time or is time using us? How can we make the most use of time?

Time-based leverage in negotiations – in negotiating, time is *the* ultimate leverage. Time-based milestones force us to agree to unpalatable terms as desperation sets in. Or, when time runs out, we prematurely terminate discussions all together. With time pressure we either give in or give up.

We need to be aware of time, as seen by both sides. We can neutralize time's adverse affect on negotiations by embodying a sense of patience. Timelessness of vision helps maintain patience during difficult negotiations.[152]

Presence – it is always helpful to be *fully present*. But can we be so "in the moment" that we lose sight of where we need to be going? One idea is:

> *Stay present, in the fabric of this instant,*
> *with threads of goal and vision.*

Presence brings creativity, insight and inspiration. Do not lose sight of the future. Use a long-term vision or goal to provide direction and purpose for each step along the way. But mostly, stay present.

Psychological time vs. clock time – in the book *The Power of Now*, Eckhart Tolle distinguishes between "psychological time" and "clock time." Psychological time is our greatest obstacle toward growth (where love is striving to take us). It is guilt and shame associated with the past or our fear of the future; both distract us from the present moment.

It is only in the midst of the present moment where we can grow.

When we do not allow ourselves to be present, the past merely gets reflected into the future and our life continues in status quo.

*Forgiveness is timeless.
It undoes the past in the present, releasing the future.*
- Unknown

Clock time on the other hand is the necessary use of time to get our jobs done. We need it in order to keep appointments, manage projects and coordinate conference calls across multiple time zones. An effective use of time is to be truly present in this moment, using clock time as a necessary tool.

Now – this instant of time is the closest we can get to *eternity* in this world. Neither the past nor the future exists; all we *ever* have is *now*.

Perfect timelessness – while working in Germany I often heard the word "perfect" spoken during our meetings. I asked, "What do you mean by the word 'perfect'? It seems different than how we use that word in the U.S." I was told, "We mean 'that is as good as it is going to get today; we can stop now.'" I like that definition. Perfection is achieved in this instant of time.

You are not guiltless in time, but in eternity.[153]
You have 'sinned' in the past, but there is no past.[154]
*Always has no direction. Time seems to go in one direction, but when you reach its end it will roll up like a long carpet spread along the past behind you, and will disappear.
As long as you believe [you are] guilty you will walk along this carpet … it is only a matter of time, and time is but an illusion.*
- A Course in Miracles

Stay in the moment; take the next right step – there are two things we need to be concerned about: the moment we are in – this instant of time – and our next step.

While taking the next right step, stay in the moment – while we are taking the next right step, it is best to stay very present. We can give ourselves a break. We don't need to be thinking about the step after this step until this step is done. We don't have to be thinking about tomorrow either. The best thing is to be very present, in this step, until this step is done. Then, *after* this step is done, think about what the following next right step is. After you finish this step, your understanding of the following right step will likely change; but you won't know until *after* you have completed *this* step.

Don't get ahead of yourself. When taking each step, relax and be present, guided by goal-based vision.

Can you imagine what it means to have no cares, no worries,
no anxieties, but merely to be perfectly calm
and quiet all the time?
Yet that is what time is for; to learn just that and nothing more.
- A Course in Miracles

Spiritual Principles in Strategic Alliances

Biography

Joe Kittel is changing the world by consulting with businesses and coaching individuals in strategic alliance management.[155] He has written the book *Spiritual Principles in Strategic Alliances: Transform Status Quo Mediocrity into Greatness*.[156] He helped found GP+S, Inc., a U.S. subsidiary of a German alliance-oriented business development consultancy. Since 1989, Joe has focused on the establishment, development and management of strategic alliances. While at HP he worked on behalf of enterprise sales, software development solutions, enterprise systems, the corporation, hosting & outsourcing services, and imaging & printing.

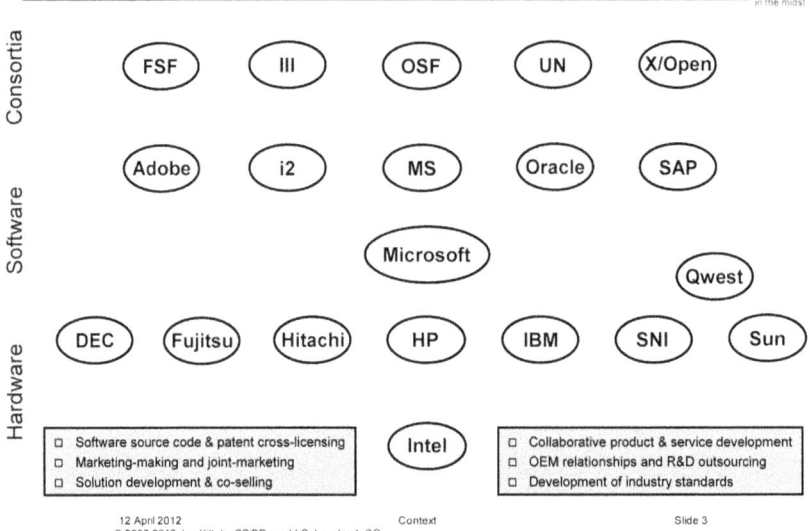

Partners and types of alliances – nearly every high-tech company and nearly every form of alliance.

Joe's philosophy is grounded in *The Program on Negotiation*, personal experience (16 years as a strategic alliance manager), coursework and independent study. He helped develop alliancing and negotiating training at Hewlett-Packard (HP) and presented at the Wharton School of Business on how to partner with Microsoft. In 1997, Joe was a member of the team the defined the Association of Strategic Alliance Professionals (ASAP's pre-Board).

In 1997, Joe helped establish HP's corporate-wide strategic alliance with Microsoft, driving collaboration in its most strategically sensitive and contentious area – UNIX/NT interoperability. Afterward, he led an HP-wide team of over 125 Microsoft alliance managers throughout HP, leading negotiations and consulting for various HP businesses. This work increased effectiveness by helping others span the strategic and cultural chasms between these two high-tech behemoths. The culmination of Joe's alliancing work at HP was the establishment of the first strategic alliance between SAP and HP's printing business (IPG) in 2005. The alliance's $300M catalyst deal was an exercise in persistence and tenacity, necessitating the embodiment and use of practical spiritual principles. This alliance is now valued at over $1B a year by HP/IPG.

Joe has received numerous awards and acknowledgements, including the following: plaque from HP for perseverance and tenacity; award from Bill Gates and Lew Platt; HP leadership and perseverance award; his book and whitepaper designated as Best Practices by the *Association of Strategic Alliance Professionals*; and a *Make a Difference Day* and *Points of Light Foundation* award for his hometown, Loveland, Colorado.

Joe graduated magna cum laude in electrical engineering (quantum electronics) from the University of Utah, EE honor society president. He has four children, two cats and lives in Loveland, Colorado.

REFERENCES

(Endnotes)

1. For a definition of "strategic alliance," see the definition in Chapter 2 – *Strategic Alliances*. For a discussion of spiritual principles, see Chapter 6 – *The Power in Simple Truths*, especially the section on Spirituality.
2. "Value" is central to alliances – it is why they exist. It is also central to this book. See "value" in Key Terms in the Appendix.
3. If you are concerned that we are talking about organized religion, refer to the section in Chapter 6 titled Question: Are We Talking About Religion?
4. For more about my life story go to www.spibr.org/joe_kittel_story.pdf.
5. For a list of books that have most influenced me, see Books Along My Path in the Appendix or go to www.spibr.org/good_books.html.
6. For more information on my five simple truths, spiritual principles or ideas, refer to Chapter 6 or go to www.spibr.org/simple_truths.html.
7. "Substantial experience" means several years, at least 3-5 years, ideally more. Alternatively, this may also mean alliance managers whose experience is already substantial; they are achieving great success without knowing why – there is something innate about them that others are interested in understanding and emulating.
8. The reason I wrote this book was to (a) collect my thoughts, (b) legitimize the concepts and (c) create a business-launching platform; it was not necessarily to sell a lot of books. I have accomplished (a) and (b) and (c) is in progress. I also wrote this to give of myself to you, to be of service, to expand my practice in Self-Obsolescence (discussed later in Chapter 8).
9. At times I will use "our Self" rather than "our self", or I will use "your Self" rather than "yourself" – this is done to emphasize the importance of our relationship with the core of us, our sacred reality, hence, the capitalization of "Self."
10. This may sound like religious zealotry; it's actually simply my personal vision for what's possible with the ideas in this book. These ideas will change the world.
11. Grandiosity is all about "me." Grandeur is all about "we." See Key Terms in the Appendix.
12. Refer to my Biography in the Appendix for more detail.

13. Content for these briefings was based on an HP-wide team I established and lead called the "Microsoft Alliance Effectiveness Team." For over two years, many of the Microsoft-affected HP business shared their insights and best practices on how to work with Microsoft. Also see Figure 8.3b that summarizes 5 years of collective work on the cultural and strategic differences between HP and Microsoft at that time.
14. SAP is the #1 business software company in the world, based in Walldorf, Germany; #3 in overall software, after Microsoft and Oracle.
15. Successes were evidenced in stock options, bonuses, raises; I also received awards, acknowledgements and plaques from a division General Manager, VP, Senior VP and two from HP's CEO and one from Microsoft's CEO.
16. See *Agents of Change* in Chapter 5.
17. My apology for profanity, but this is a literal quote, and these words exquisitely make the point.
18. At the risk of bringing childhood psychoanalysis into this, being an excessively competitive egomaniac makes a lot of sense. I was the youngest of four boys with an alcoholic father, where love seemed linked to how successful we were in competitive swimming.
19. See *Focus Collective Attention on Value* in Chapter 8.
20. In November of 2010, Friedreich's Ataxia took the life of my oldest child, Aaron, at the age of 33. To learn more about FA, go to **www.curefa.org**.
21. It seems there are two ways to view anything, from either a *fear*-based or *love*-based position. *Competition* is, "I will prove I am better when I beat you or put you out of business." It is about "me vs. you." *Inspiration* is "You make me want to be a better person"; it is about "we."
22. Wherever possible, "The Infinite" is used in this book, rather than "God." In quoted text "God" is retained if used by the author. Other words could include Higher Power, nature or the Universe. It has been my experience that these relationships (with The Infinite, Self and others) all deepen *simultaneously*. In fact, it seems like they *must* deepen in parallel, empirical evidence of *Oneness*.
23. For more discussion on how spiritual principles are helpful to strategic alliance managers, see Chapter 7 – *The Value of Spirituality in Business Relationships, and* in particular, the section on *Personal Value*.
24. Incremental revenue in an alliance has an emphasis on "unique," meaning that the *only* way this revenue can be obtained is via a business

References (Endnotes)

relationship. We should not ignore revenue, but we should not stop there as we look for value in an alliance. We are not "blinded" by revenue; we look "beyond" it to other forms of tangible and intangible value. There is more to an alliance than revenue. And it is in the invisible and timeless forms of value that near-term tangible value is conceived.

25 *Simple Rules for Making Alliances Work* by Jonathan Hughes and Jeff Weiss, Harvard Business Review, November 2007.

26 The use of the word "love" may seem inappropriate in business. It is used to describe a universal force that compels us all to grow. As I see it, growth is nearly synonymous with love. See *Key Terms* in the Appendix.

27 *Managing Alliances for Business Results: Lessons Learned from Leading Companies* by Jeff Weiss, Sara Keen and Stuart Kliman; Vantage Partners, LLC. A 2006 study of alliancing in 93 companies from various industries: healthcare, high-technology (computers & IT), manufacturing, pharmaceuticals and professional services. Except where stated otherwise, this report is the basis for statistics in Chapter 3. Also, by "fail" we mean failed outright or only achieved the alliance's initial goals, i.e., there was significant value-creating potential that was left untapped in the alliance.

28 *Managing Alliance Relationships: Ten Key Corporate Capabilities – A Cross-Industry Study of How to Build and Manage Successful Alliances* by Danny Ertel, Jeff Weiss and Laura Judy Visioni; Vantage Partners, LLC.

29 See the section on *Simplicity* in Chapter 6.

30 *The Program on Negotiation* is a multi-university consortium started in 1983 at Harvard Law School, with participation from Harvard, MIT and Tufts universities. PON is focused on developing the theory and practice of effective negotiating and dispute resolution. Ref: **www.pon.harvard.edu**.

31 Trust – reliance, consistency, integrity, confidence, dependability. Honesty is related to trust, but it's really an outcome of trust.

32 "Confrontation" means to openly, lovingly and collaboratively face something *in* a relationship, *between* people or companies. To "co-front" a tough issue. "Conflict" is different; it is about attacking a *person* or *company*, not the issue. Read *Building Trust in Strategic Alliances: enabling greater value* for more discussion on how confrontation calls for trust, and so trust comes (**www.spibr.org/Building_trust_and_value_in_alliances.pdf**).

33 *Managing Alliances for Business Results: Lessons Learned from Leading Companies* by Jeff Weiss, Sara Keen and Stuart Kliman; Vantage Partners, LLC.

34. Ref: www.shrm.org.
35. *The Psychology of Success* by Dobbins, Richard, Pettman, Barrie O.; published in 1992 by Equal Opportunities International.
36. See *Thoughts on Metrics* in the Appendix.
37. See Chapter 8 – *Some Spiritual Practices in Strategic Alliancing*.
38. See *Awareness* in Chapter 8 for a discussion on holistic listening.
39. Ref: www.pon.harvard.edu.
40. Remember the text in the box; you will see it later in this book. This sentence forms the basis for practical spirituality, further developed in Chapter 6 – *The Power in Simple Truths*.
41. Also consider reading *Role of Strategic Alliance Manager: a unique, holistic and empowering perspective* available at **www.spibr.org/strategic_alliance_mgmt.pdf**. Written after this book, this paper expands and focuses on key concepts related to role of alliance manager.
42. See *Thoughts on Metrics* in the Appendix 10.3.
43. Addictive behavior is using something to distract us from looking at the truth because looking at the truth can be uncomfortable. Most deeply we use additions to avoid facing the truth of *who we are*.
44. A "NOP" is a programming step in assembly language (very basic machine-level computer programming). It is short for "No OPeration." A NOP is something that does nothing at all, by design.
45. Ref: *The Program on Negotiation* at **www.pon.harvard.edu**.
46. See *Self-Obsolescence* in Chapter 8.
47. *Change the World*, written by an MBA professor, explicitly and directly straddles spirituality and business. Buy it, read it, live it!
48. 16 years as an alliance manager. See *Biography* in the Appendix.
49. See *Self-Obsolescence* in Chapter 8.
50. John 10:34 in the *Bible*.
51. Refer to Chapter 6 – *The Power in Simple Truths* and Chapter 8 – *Some Spiritual Practices in Strategic Alliancing*.
52. As we explicitly focus on spirituality it may be worth referring back to the *Spiritual Disclaimer* at the beginning of Chapter 1.
53. *Sermon on the Mount* by Emmet Fox, pg. 123.
54. See *Thoughts on Two Thoughts Systems* in the Appendix.
55. "Ego" in this book differs some from traditional use. It describes part of our thinking grounded in fear and separation. See *Key Terms* in the Appendix.

References (Endnotes)

56. See Chapters 2 and 3 for a discussion on the complexities of our job and the addictive nature of complexity.
57. How can we "prove" truths or "prove" the value of spirituality? Often we see in another something they cannot see in themselves. And others see in us what we cannot see. Life is "a we thing." See *Personal Value* in Chapter 7.
58. See *Biography* in the Appendix.
59. *Narcotics Anonymous* basic text, page 87.
60. See *Books Along My Path* in the Appendix for a list of readings that have impacted my spiritual path and the *Biography* in the Appendix.
61. Send e-mail to **joe@spibr.org**. We intend to establish a forum for practical, experiential sharing.
62. See *Key Terms* in the Appendix for definitions of ego and spirit.
63. Clearly, trade secrets are necessary and need to be protected in business.
64. See *Thoughts on Two Thought Systems* in the Appendix for a more detailed discussion of these ideas.
65. The "Golden Rule" is a common principle in many religions, the ethic of reciprocity – love another as Self. "Karma" is similar – what we do in life, what we do to others, comes back to us.
66. See *Thoughts on Time* in the Appendix.
67. Ref: **www.strengthsfinder.com**.
68. Ref: "Pray in … all occasions" (Eph. 6:18) and "… pray about everything" (Phil. 4:5).
69. *Evidence of Correlations Between Distant Intentionality and Brain Function in Recipients: A Functional Magnet Resonance Imaging Analysis* in The Journal of Alternative and Complementary Medicine, Vol. 11, Nov. 6, 2005, pp. 965-971 (this article can be found at **http://www.spibr.org/2005_JofACM_Distant_Intentionality_and_Brain_Function_by_Achterberg_et_al.pdf**).
70. Previously, I committed to use "The Infinite" rather than "God." In this section, for brevity and succinctness, I revert back to "old ways" and use this 3-letter word, rather than a 2-word phrase, all pointing to the same idea. I hope the use of "God" does not offend you.
71. 1 John 4:8 in the *Bible*. See also the definition of "love" in *Key Terms* in the Appendix.
72. In the Bible it says the most important commandment is to love God and love your neighbor as yourself. Mark 12:30-31.

73. The 2nd Law of Thermodynamics – over time, randomness increases and energy decreases. Things fall apart into lower levels of order. Eventually all things fall into disarray. This is a "universal law," especially in closed systems. Well, the universe is not closed, and love is the counter to the universal force, entropy. Otherwise, why do we humans even exist?

74. *Narcotics Anonymous* basic text, pg 85.

75. See Figures 4.6 and 4.7 for review.

76. See the quote about "home" toward the end of the section titled *Transforming an Alliance into a Productive Community* in Chapter 8.

77. See *Two Thought Systems* in Chapter 6 and *Thoughts on Two Thought Systems* in the Appendix.

78. See *Thoughts on Meditation* in the Appendix. Regularly practice meditation or simply being quiet.

79. Steve Job's commencement speech to Stanford University's class of 2005.

80. Actually, the writing of this book to you is an act of self-obsolescence. The danger of this act is perceived to be career danger. It flies in the face of a common adage in business, "Knowledge is power, so keep it to yourself." My experience has been the opposite. As I give freely of my knowledge and wisdom, it grows. It grows in the process of giving (in the act of teaching) and in receiving back from others.

81. Paraphrased from *The Power of Now* by Eckhart Tolle.

82. *Simple Rules for Making Alliances Work* by Jonathan Hughes and Jeff Weiss, Harvard Business Review, November 2007. And the Association of Strategic Alliance Professionals, 2007 Summit. Also, alliances are the most challenging form of business relationships. Effectiveness-improving lessons learned in alliancing can be applied to other forms of business relationships.

83. *Managing Alliances for Business Results: Lessons Learned from Leading Companies* by Jeff Weiss, Sara Keen and Stuart Kliman; Vantage Partners, LLC. Survey done in 2006.

84. Here's the logic: with a 57% failure rate and 40% of failures caused by relationship that means that 22.8% of alliances fail due to relationship issues. If instead 30% of the failures were due to relationship, that would reduce alliance failures due to relationship issues down to 17.1% – a 5.7 percentage point reduction in overall alliance failure rate.

85. Review *The Insightful Intersect – Relationship & People | Attitude & Mindset* and the *Summary* in Chapter 4.

References (Endnotes)

86 If you think such a world would be *less* intense, see *Negotiating with a Spiritual Teacher – Negotiating with The Infinite* in Chapter 5.

87 *Alcoholics Anonymous* pg 49.

88 Many of these practices and others will be expounded upon in whitepapers. Visit **www.spibr.org** or send an e-mail to **joe@spibr.org** for a current list of publications or to provide your input on these or other spiritual practices in strategic alliances.

89 "Meeting" is all-inclusive, encompassing conferences, conference calls, webcasts, any gathering of people, even just two people.

90 *Finding Flow* by Mihaly Csikszenthihalyi.

91 See *Thoughts on Meditation* in the Appendix.

92 Confrontation is further developed in the next section *Be Lovingly Confrontational*.

93 *The Power of Now* by Eckhart Tolle, pages 126-127 – The Art of Listening. The words "the *Being* of the other person" can be replaced with "the *truth within*" or "the *truth about* the other person."

94 The spiritual practice of listening to the voice of the collective is discussed further in Chapter 8; see *Focus Collective Attention on Value*.

95 As I see it, this flow of life which affects people and events is synonymous with love, spirit, or God. This is the force in and of the universe which counters entropy and compels everything and everyone to grow. Look carefully at the bubbles in Figure 6.4.

96 HP's printing business (IPG) measured product lifecycles in six-month increments. To help HP/IPG to accept SAP's decades-long time perspective was another area of "time-awareness" I had to deal with.

97 In this situation HP had commercial software that HP was willing to license to SAP. SAP could then incorporate HP's software into their product. For software vendors, especially SAP at the time, being "open" to consider such OEM relationships is a huge change, a strategic shift.

98 NetWeaver is SAP's application-integration middleware. Adobe was the first major software vendor to license (or OEM) their commercial software to SAP for inclusion in NetWeaver.

99 See the HP/SAP press release at **http://www.spibr.org/060514_HP-SAP_CPM_Press_Release.pdf**. The $300M valuation was based on HP's estimated leveraged business (systems, devices, services and consumables) calculated over HP's planning horizon.

100 The collectively listening aspect of awareness is more fully developed

in the section on *Focus Collective Attention on Value* in Chapter 8. The importance of *listening* warrants repetition.

101 By "space-less" we mean, to see events occur that span across various organizations, across companies, across ecosystems.

102 See *Key Terms* in the Appendix for a definition of "love."

103 Dealing with the elephant can seem to have more down-side than up-side career opportunity. Removing an elephant takes a lot of work. "Fire fighters" are more politically visible than "fire preventers" (I apologize for mixing metaphors.)

104 Every industry has examples of such partners. When you mention their name people are struck with awe and respect for the alliance manager who has to *deal* with them. In high-technology in the 80s and 90s, that was Microsoft. In retail, I suspect it is Wal-Mart. People just accept that "life is tough" in these alliances, and no one bothers dealing with root cause issues.

105 In business there are some issues that must be kept hidden, like trade secrets. Intellectual property needs to be protected. What we are talking about here are issues hidden not for protection, but issues hidden out of fear. Things we literally hate to face.

106 The 4th Step is the inventory "*We* made a searching and fearless moral inventory of ourselves." The 5th Step is the *un-hiding* part, "*We* admitted to God, to ourselves, and to another human being (a trusted other) the exact nature of our wrongs (we look at it)." Ref: *Narcotics Anonymous*, W.S.O., Inc. Italics added for emphasis, parenthetic statements added for clarity.

107 See *Two Thought Systems* in Chapter 6 and *Thoughts on Two Thought Systems* in the Appendix.

108 In this case the metaphorical concept is used to *introduce* the idea that *we* **are** light. Our mind *is* light.

109 Ultraviolet light is used to sterilize tools in medical facilities. UV light also disinfects wastewater and drinking water.

110 "Self" is capitalized to denote our divine core; the truth, light and love at our center.

111 If we want to fundamentally transform how alliances are done, if we want to continue trying to "do the impossible with nothing," it seems like being a "miracle worker" hits the mark in describing our job.

112 The whitepaper *Simply Focus on Incremental Value and Value-impediments: transforming a strategic alliance through simplicity* more

References (Endnotes)

thoroughly discusses this practice; it's available at **www.spibr.org/2-slide_methodology.pdf**.

113   Ref: **www.pon.harvard.edu**. *The Program on Negotiation* is a multi-university consortium dedicated to the practice of negotiating and dispute resolution with representation from Harvard University, Harvard Law School, Massachusetts Institute of Technology and Tufts University. Refer to my Biography at the end of the Appendix to understand my experiential basis for these ideas.

114   Focusing collective attention directly builds upon *Awareness* and *Be Lovingly Confrontational* discussed in Chapter 8. Deep listening forms the foundation of this practice.

115   Discussed in Chapter 8 in the section on *Awareness*.

116   Given the slide's simple clear focus on value, it circulated within SAP and gained support. It was "simply a matter of time."

117   Revisit Figure 8.2 – *Timeless Awareness*.

118   See **www.vantagepartners.com**. Vantage Partners are focused on helping companies negotiate and manage alliances.

119   Rather than using "him/her" I am simply using an all-inclusive "he." Besides, *he* often *is* the one who is devious and/or incompetent.

120   From time to time other factors will be as dominant as culture and strategy. For example, technical, legal or regulatory details can create challenges in a working relationship. If something affects the *working* relationship, that issue will get captured, in a *practical* manner, when we deeply listen and understand *perspective* – perspective of self and perspective of other.

121   In 1998-99, the Wharton School of Business assessed the HP/Microsoft alliance by sampling from among >150 initiatives. They determined that our two corporate cultures differed more radically than any other two high-technology companies. Microsoft was "the Green Beret – Special Forces – kill and destroy," and HP was "the Boy Scouts – naively doing good."

122   The slide's content was developed between 1997 through 2002 while establishing and managing the HP/Microsoft corporate alliance and working in various HP businesses. Also see *Simple Rules for Making Alliances Work* by Jonathan Hughes and Jeff Weiss in November 2007 *Harvard Business Review*.

123   Microsoft Exchange Server is an e-mail messaging and collaboration software application that runs on the backbone computers, or servers, in

Spiritual Principles in Strategic Alliances

a network. Basically this type of application makes e-mail happen, often unbeknownst to the actual users of e-mail.

124 Consider the impact that digital technology and the Internet are having on the music entertainment ecosystem. If you managed the alliance between Apple iTunes and RIAA (Recording Industry Association of America) or Universal Music Group, you would be involved with complex strategic decisions with far-reaching ecosystem-wide impact.

125 In the Apple/RIAA/UMG alliance example, these issues could be around technology for restricting digital rights, dealing with Napster (treat them as friend or foe?), licensing rights and fees, assessing consumer trends, collaboration with Microsoft (friend and foe), riding the wave of disruptive technologies (using examples from other ecosystems), etc..

126 In Figure 8.3c this is illustrated for ISVs – independent software vendors, developing middleware and application software.

127 See definition of value in the Appendix, *Key Terms*.

128 See *The Negotiator Role* discussed in Chapter 5. Attend *The Program on Negotiation* at Harvard, MIT & Tufts Universities **www.pon.harvard.edu** – arguably the best negotiating training for alliance managers in the world.

129 See *Negotiating with your Greatest Spiritual Teacher – negotiating with The Universe* in Chapter 5.

130 Two simple slides covering (a) incremental value and (b) value-impediments were developed in Chapter 8 in the section titled *Focus Collective Attention on Value*. That work is directly leverageable to and a critical precursor for negotiating.

131 These concepts come from *The Program on Negotiation* and the book *Getting to Yes* by Fisher and Ury.

132 See *Two Thought Systems* in Chapter 6 and *Thoughts on Two Thought Systems* in the Appendix.

133 See Chapter 6 – *The Power in Simple Truths*.

134 See *Key Terms* in the Appendix for more discussion about love. We are not talking about romantic love.

135 Chapter 6 – *The Power in Simple Truths*.

136 Clearly we need to protect intellectual property and trade secrets. These are not the ideas we suggest be given away. The ideas we should be freely giving are around alliancing and relationships.

137 We may have fears that some people will steal or hoard our alliancing ideas or take advantage of us. My response to that fear is, "take advantage

References (Endnotes)

of me and my ideas as much as you like; that is what I am here for." But you don't need to steal what I freely give.

138 There is deep fear as we confront greatness and success. Perhaps revisit *Assessing and Changing Attitude & Mindset* in Chapter 6 – reread the quotes mentioned in items 3 and 4.

139 An alternative and even deeper quote from the same source: "Yet there is another interpretation of relationships that transcends the concept of loss of *power* completely. … What you find difficult to accept is the fact that, like your Father, *you* are an idea. And like Him, you can *give yourself* completely, *wholly without loss and only gain.*"

140 The concept of "productive community" comes from *Change the World* by Robert Quinn. Based on my personal experiences, Quinn's concepts are applied to the role of alliance manager and the structure of a strategic alliance team.

141 See the definition of "fear" in *Key terms* in the Appendix. Also, revisit the quotes on openness and fearlessness toward the end of Chapter 6.

142 I consciously and voluntarily chose to leave my "dream alliance" in July 2005 for the greater good. This decision was driven by the motivation to be of maximal service to my world. I could not imagine where within HP I could be of service. I had worked in nearly every HP business, and the role of alliance manager was changing. It was becoming less service-oriented and less focused on long-term value-creation. I chose to leave in order to allow the alliance to grow and so that I could be of greater personal service to the world. Unbeknownst to me this had huge positive impact on many of the players in the alliance, as well as for me personally. It was simply a matter of time.

143 See *Acknowledgements*, just after title page.

144 From *A Return to Love* by Marianne Williamson, more fully quoted in Chapter 6 in the section titled *Assess and Changing Attitude & Mindset*.

145 See *Thoughts on Two Thought Systems* in the Appendix.

146 This love is analogous to the water in Figure 6.4 - *Spirituality*; look carefully at the bubbles in that picture. The water represents the spirit within us and between us. Also check out www.spibr.org/love_is.html.

147 From *The Power of Now* by Eckhart Tolle.

148 "Egoic mind" means thoughts based on a sense of separation – separation from spirit, from God and from others. Such thoughts are grounded in fear: a scarcity mindset, me vs. you, your win is my loss, etc. Most of our

thoughts are egoic thoughts. They are focused on problems; in fact, these thoughts *are* the problem. By increased consciousness or mindfulness developed through meditative work, we become increasingly aware of our ego-based thoughts; and because the ego does not like being observed, these thoughts simply fade away.

149 See *Key Terms* in the Appendix for a definition of "ego" and "spirit."

150 For a simpler version of this table go to **www.spibr.org/Two_thoughts_one_choice.pdf**.

151 See *Be an Illuminating Mirror* in Chapter 8.

152 See *Awareness* in Chapter 8. A vision of timeless awareness brings patience. Also, see the section titled *Focus Collective Attention on Value* in Chapter 8. Getting a clear collective view of incremental value is our goal.

153 This instant of time, this moment we are in right now, is the closest we'll get to eternity in this world.

154 "Sinned" means to have erred. It is an archery phrase, meaning your arrow missed the bull's eye; you missed the mark.

155 For other perspectives on Joe read **www.spibr.org/joe_kittel_story.pdf** (2 pgs) and **www.spibr.org/Joe_Kittel_resume.pdf** (3 pgs).

156 Excerpts from this book have been selected and published as an *ASAP Best Practice Bulletin*, a monthly membership bulletin for the Association of Strategic Alliance Professionals (**www.strategic-alliances.org**).

www.ingramcontent.com/pod-product-compliance
Lightning Source LLC
Chambersburg PA
CBHW051121160426
43195CB00014B/2293